M000302231

"Schwabish and team are master communicators! And *Elevate the Debate* masterfully explains how to bring your scholarship and data-driven research out of the library, off the page, and into the eyes and minds of those who can put it to good use."
—David Autor, Ford Professor of Economics,
Massachusetts Institute of Technology

"Being an expert is both a privilege and a responsibility. So often researchers struggle to clearly frame their work in a way a larger audience can appreciate. *Elevate the Debate* lays out easy-to-follow steps that will help the wonkiest of wonks break down their research and clearly explain why their work matters. If you wish more people could appreciate why your work is important, check this book out."
—Dan Gorenstein, host and executive producer of *Tradeoffs*,
a health policy podcast

"*Elevate the Debate* is the scholar's handbook to bridging the divide with policymakers and making a real impact with one's research. The research report is yesterday's tool for dissemination; the infographic is today's. The Urban Institute team clearly and artfully guides academics in identifying their audiences and visualizing results in new, more media-friendly ways that hold great promise for improving evidence-based policy and practice."
—Carolyn Heinrich, Patricia and Rodes Hart Professor of Public
Policy, Education and Economics, Vanderbilt University

"Scholars spend years learning how to conduct research but rarely are taught to convey insights effectively. This book offers a thoughtful and accessible way to fill that gap by helping researchers to identify an audience, to use more than one medium, and to tailor content, visuals, and tone to broaden their reach."
—Ellen Meara, Professor of Health Economics and Policy,
Department of Health Policy and Management,
Harvard T.H. Chan School of Public Health

"In an age of increasing disinformation and noise, it's crucial that scientists, researchers, and educators of all types get their message out with simplicity and clarity. Evidence-based thinking and communicating have never been more important than they are today. This may be the most important book you read this year!"

—Garr Reynolds, author of *Presentation Zen* and Professor of Management at Kansai Gaidai University

"Data without communication is just data. This essential guide shows you how to transform those numbers into something real and vital that can have true impact. If you want to change the world with data, this guide is a great place to start."

—Simon Rogers, Google

"At a time when the world struggles to separate fact from fiction in our media and information, there are few more important endeavors than guiding researchers and scholars in disseminating their work. This exceptional volume from the Urban Institute is an essential and timely resource for doing just that. Here's hoping it is widely read and absorbed!"

—Jimmy Soni, award-winning author of *A Mind at Play: How Claude Shannon Invented the Information Age*

"This book is the essential how-to guide for researchers and analysts who intend to be relevant. Getting your message into the right hands doesn't happen by accident!"

—Tom Terry, CEO of the Terry Group

"*Elevate the Debate* is a fabulous new book that offers to teach researchers how to communicate our work to get attention from multiple audiences. This volume takes the importance of a good presentation as a start and goes on to help researchers and analysts to communicate data, research, and analysis to different audiences. It is accessible, clearly written, and a very important tool to increase the use of our work to improve policy formation. I hope it is widely read and followed."

—Barbara L. Wolfe, Richard A. Easterlin Professor of Economics, Population Health Sciences, and Public Affairs, University of Wisconsin–Madison

Elevate the Debate

Elevate the Debate

A Multilayered Approach to
Communicating Your Research

Edited by
Jonathan Schwabish

WILEY

© 2020 by John Wiley & Sons, Inc. All rights reserved.

Published by John Wiley & Sons, Inc., Hoboken, New Jersey.
Published simultaneously in Canada.

No part of this publication may be reproduced, stored in a retrieval system, or transmitted in any form or by any means, electronic, mechanical, photocopying, recording, scanning, or otherwise, except as permitted under Section 107 or 108 of the 1976 United States Copyright Act, without either the prior written permission of the Publisher, or authorization through payment of the appropriate per-copy fee to the Copyright Clearance Center, Inc., 222 Rosewood Drive, Danvers, MA 01923, (978) 750-8400, fax (978) 646-8600, or on the Web at www.copyright.com. Requests to the Publisher for permission should be addressed to the Permissions Department, John Wiley & Sons, Inc., 111 River Street, Hoboken, NJ 07030, (201) 748-6011, fax (201) 748-6008, or online at www.wiley.com/go/permissions.

Limit of Liability/Disclaimer of Warranty: While the publisher and author have used their best efforts in preparing this book, they make no representations or warranties with respect to the accuracy or completeness of the contents of this book and specifically disclaim any implied warranties of merchantability or fitness for a particular purpose. No warranty may be created or extended by sales representatives or written sales materials. The advice and strategies contained herein may not be suitable for your situation. You should consult with a professional where appropriate. Neither the publisher nor author shall be liable for any loss of profit or any other commercial damages, including but not limited to special, incidental, consequential, or other damages.

For general information on our other products and services or for technical support, please contact our Customer Care Department within the United States at (800) 762-2974, outside the United States at (317) 572-3993, or fax (317) 572-4002.

Wiley publishes in a variety of print and electronic formats and by print-on-demand. Some material included with standard print versions of this book may not be included in e-books or in print-on-demand. If this book refers to media such as a CD or DVD that is not included in the version you purchased, you may download this material at http://booksupport.wiley.com. For more information about Wiley products, visit www.wiley.com.

Library of Congress Cataloging-in-Publication Data:

Names: Schwabish, Jonathan A., editor.
Title: Elevate the debate : a multilayered approach to communicating your research / edited by Jonathan Schwabish.
Description: First edition. | Hoboken, New Jersey : John Wiley & Sons, Inc., [2020] | Includes bibliographical references and index.
Identifiers: LCCN 2019046227 (print) | LCCN 2019046228 (ebook) | ISBN 9781119620013 (paperback) | ISBN 9781119620037 (adobe pdf) | ISBN 9781119620020 (epub)
Subjects: LCSH: Sociology, Urban—Research—United States. | Urban policy—Research—United States. | Communication in city planning—United States.
Classification: LCC HT123 .E44 2020 (print) | LCC HT123 (ebook) | DDC 307.76072/073—dc23
LC record available at https://lccn.loc.gov/2019046227
LC ebook record available at https://lccn.loc.gov/2019046228

Cover image and design: Allison Feldman

Printed in the United States of America

V10016617_122719

Contents

Acknowledgments

The chapters in this book were developed from a series of workshops that the Urban Institute Communications Department conducted between 2016 and 2019. Workshop participants hailed from diverse fields: housing, international development, social work, labor economics, healthcare, and more. Feedback was unanimously positive, and we were inspired to empower more researchers by putting those lessons in words.

We are indebted to the researchers at the Urban Institute whose dedication to their scholarship and their collaborative spirit has helped make Urban a trusted resource for thought leaders, academics, practitioners, journalists, and policymakers. We also thank our current and former Urban colleagues who supported this project directly: Rob Abare, Fiona Blackshaw, Ben Chartoff, Matt Chingos, Mary Cunningham, Allison Feldman, Dan Fowler, Martha Galvez, Heather Hahn, Rachel Kenney, Arlene Corbin Lewis, Jeffrey Lin, Rhiannon Newman, Sheryl Pardo, Archana Pyati, Brittney Spinner, Jerry Ta, Alex Tilsley, John Wehmann, and Sarita Williams.

We are grateful to the president of the Urban Institute, Sarah Rosen Wartell, for her leadership; for believing in accessible, engaging research; and for providing a vision that inspires us to "elevate the debate" every day.

The most important contribution to this book comes from the authors, all of whom are experts in their fields of communicating research and analysis in different ways across different mediums and platforms. They all share a belief in the importance of using data, facts, and research to help improve public policy, communities, and lives.

—Jonathan Schwabish

Preface

The Urban Institute is a nonprofit research institution located in Washington, DC. It was founded in 1968 to study the nation's urban problems and evaluate the Great Society initiatives of the Lyndon B. Johnson administration. Today, Urban comprises more than 500 social scientists, economists, mathematicians, demographers, data scientists, policy experts, and communicators. At our core, we believe good decisions are shaped by facts, rather than ideology, have the power to improve public policy and practice, strengthen communities, redirect the way businesses think and operate, and transform people's lives for the better. Our research is not done for the sake of research or for a handful of other scholars; it is conducted to serve as a catalyst for change in perception, thought, and action.

Urban's Communication Department began to grow rapidly in 2013, evolving to better help Urban connect with other researchers, policymakers, practitioners, the public, and the press. With a refreshed brand identity and transformed digital presence, Urban began pioneering new ways to bring research to life. Today, a modernized approach and institute serves as a model for other nonprofits and organizations.

As Urban's communication efforts began to bear fruit, the team began to host trainings—internally and externally—on a range of topics including media relations, blogging, social media, data visualization, presentation skills, and translating research for policymakers.

At the request of a major foundation, we rolled all these together into a daylong session to equip researchers with the tools they need. Today, we offer these personalized trainings to a range of academic researchers and organizations seeking more meaningful impact for their important work. In this book, we capture our overviews, tips, and tactics so they can be yours to remember and apply.

———————————

When Bridget Lowell, Urban's Chief Communications Officer kicks off our Research to Policy Boot Camp, she starts with a simple question: "How many of you have felt frustrated when working with a reporter or a marketing communications staffer?"

Immediately, almost all hands go up

The second question she asks is, "How many times have you invested significant time and energy to painstakingly help nonexperts understand your issue, only to have them publish stories in which they get it all wrong?"

Most hands stay up

Whether at an academic institution, nonprofit organization, or government agency, researchers far too often feel that their work is ignored or misrepresented. Many feel that doing a better job communicating their work is outside their skill set or not worth their time. At Urban, we feel just the opposite. We feel that people who have dedicated their time to conduct objective, rigorous research can also effectively communicate that work to whatever audience they want to reach. The same communications toolkit we follow can be applied by any organization that seeks to share research-based information and rally audiences to thoughtfully consider a point of debate and drive the correct decision-making to solve a problem. In that way, the techniques we have developed at Urban may be used by researchers and thought leaders of all types, *elevating the debate* inside and outside their organizations.

It takes time. It takes effort. It takes skill. But it can be done, and this book will help you do so. Our goal in this book is to take you through the journey of effectively communicating your work to your audience across eight different subject areas. Together, they will help you find and reach your audience. There are a variety of payoffs to doing so: reaching a broader audience; having an impact on policy; finding new collaborators; finding new data; and finding new funders, to name just a few.

This book is organized in eight chapters to help you on your way to better research communication.

1. **Introduction.** How do you identify your target audience, and how do you argue the importance of better communication? Bridget Lowell lays out the case for why better communication is imperative to prove that facts matter.

2. **Audience outreach.** Who are the policymakers, decision-makers, and influencers who can help circulate your work or connect you with other potential collaborators, groups, and funders? Amy Elsbree and Amy Peake show you how to be deliberate about who you are trying to reach and how you will reach them.

3. **Data visualization.** How do you create visuals and graphs that do a better job communicating your findings? Jonathan Schwabish discusses different graph types and some of the best practices to visualize your data.

4. **Presentations.** What are the strategies and approaches to giving presentations that engage an audience and help them use your research? In this chapter, Schwabish discusses how to plan, design, and deliver an effective presentation.

5. **Blogging.** How do you get your message into the hands of those who can use it to make better decisions? In this chapter, Nicole Levins shows why blogging matters for communicating research, and what you need to know to get started.

6. **Media relations.** How can you talk to reporters about your work, engage them, and have your work mentioned and cited in

newspapers, blogs, radio, and podcasts? In this chapter, Stu Kantor gives you specific strategies to approach your next interview with calm and confidence.

7. **Social media.** What are the strategies and best practices to use social media platforms like Twitter and Facebook to connect and converse with new and influential audiences? David Connell provides you with the techniques you need to engage on social media platforms in a way that feels comfortable and productive, and does not distract from the important work you're already doing.

8. **Impact plan.** With all this information and tools now at your fingertips, how do you pull it all together? In this final chapter, Kate Villarreal shows you how to build an overarching communications strategy that weaves together the tactics and products into a single, focused plan.

Together, these chapters will provide you with the basic, practical strategies to be your own communications manager. See our webpage for more information and downloadable resources and worksheets: https://www.urban.org/ElevatetheDebateBook.

As a team, we are committed to helping researchers and other data-driven knowledge seekers do a better job communicating their research and reaching their desired audiences. We are sharing our tools, techniques, and strategies because we believe that more and better communication of important research can lead to better outcomes.

We hope President Lyndon Johnson would be proud of the independent institute he commissioned in 1968, one that promised "to give us the power through knowledge to help solve the problem that weighs heavily on the hearts and minds of all of us—the problem of the American city and its people." He hoped the Urban Institute would fill a real need by "bridging the gulf between the lonely scholar in search of truth and the decision-maker in search of progress." We hope this book will advance today's scholars and decisionmakers on that journey.

chapter one

Why Research Needs a Big Audience

Bridget Lowell

If you're like most researchers, you question the value of communicating your work to a broader audience. It's fair to be skeptical. Maybe it seems trivial. Maybe you've been burned by a reporter who completely misunderstood your findings, despite your having spent an hour on the phone explaining them. Maybe your results got distorted by a well-meaning blogger who doesn't quite understand what a confidence interval is. Maybe your peers or department chair sneered at you for blogging or tweeting, saying your time was better spent writing for academic journals.

I get it. I've heard all these complaints, and more. My goal—and our goal throughout this book—is to demonstrate that being a successful scholar today requires that you share your insights *beyond* the academic community. After all, what value is your research if it doesn't connect to the very world it is trying to influence and change? Great research—whether it comes from the academic community, non-profit research organizations, or thought leaders in business and elsewhere—needs a *plan* to find different and wider audiences that can expand its impact.

We will arm you with the necessary tools to translate your work on your own terms, telling the reader and user how to interpret your findings. After reading this book, you will be inspired and equipped to use traditional and digital media to your advantage, and you will never sneer—or be sneered at—again for communicating your work to the world.

We wrote this guide for the converted and the skeptics because, frankly, the research community can no longer afford not to participate in the conversation. Evidence-based thinking needs to push its way deeper into all institutions and organizations so that insight and keen observation have legs to stand on everywhere. Your goal should be to take the results of your research into all conversations and ultimately drive sound critical thinking, decision-making, and problem-solving.

It's up to you to prove that facts matter. And to make them count.

The environment for facts, science, and information began a radical shift even before "alternative facts" and "fake news" entered our lexicon. Respect for institutions—the ones that have typically been the sources for widely agreed-upon facts—has been eroding for years. A March 2019 poll by the Pew Research Center found that "majorities of Americans had not too much or no confidence in the news media, business leaders or elected officials to act in the public interest." Other surveys also find declining trust in business, media, government, and nongovernment organizations (NGOs) globally and in the United States. A June 2018 Gallup poll shows public confidence is lowest in Congress and media organizations, but "no institution has shown a larger drop in confidence over the past three years than higher education." Gallup found the decline in trust in academia was steepest among self-identified Republicans, but Democrats and independents expressed less confidence as well.

This is perhaps best summarized by what former United Kingdom Justice Secretary Michael Gove said in the fallout after the Brexit vote in the United Kingdom: "People in this country have had enough of experts."

Federally elected officials, themselves often ranked among the least-trusted, are hardly embracing evidence as they develop and vote on legislation. In 2017, some members of Congress went so far as to stop relying on the objective, nonpartisan legislative analyses of the Congressional Budget Office, which had long been upheld as the definitive source for budget and economic estimates.

So, the bad news is that the stakes are high, facts are endangered, and people conducting serious research and analysis can't afford to sit on the sidelines. To ensure that research is factored into today's most important decisions, researchers must engage in today's fast-evolving policy ecosystem.

The good news is that it's never been easier to do so.

Never has it been easier for researchers to directly set the terms of debate. Never have scholars had this much control over how their evidence is presented and disseminated. Never have people been so well equipped to democratize data and put information directly into users' hands for thought and consideration, and possible action around evidence-based thinking.

Today's consumers of information have access, transparency, and the opportunity to personalize information and understand what it means for their own communities like never before. This is how we will demonstrate as a research community that facts do indeed matter, and they matter more than ever.

Be Strategic: Set Goals for Impact

Too many scholars and analysts write a report, memo, or blog post and expect that by virtue of its quality alone, it will find an audience and generate positive impact. But that's not how it works in today's crowded landscape of content, research, and data. Impact is earned not through dissemination at the report's conclusion, but through intention and careful planning at its inception. Ideally, your outreach plan should coincide with your research design. You should start by asking, *What questions am I answering, and what problems am I solving with this research? For whom and to what end?*

Effective communications and outreach strategies always start with questions, not findings. Questions such as: Who can benefit from my research? How might it improve their decisions? How does my audience consume information, and how can I present my findings in a way that works for them?

Meet People Where They Are

In this book, our team provides you with the tools and tactics to get evidence directly into the hands of people who need it—whether they know it or not.

The first step is to define and understand your audience, then adjust your product to your audience's needs. Your audience should never be "the general public," a meaningless description reviled by marketers. Your audience is the consumer of your work: the individual empowered to take action upon engaging with it. A fellow scholar at a university might be eager to dig into your 150-page report, but a staffer on Capitol Hill or a busy CEO might only have time for the topline findings during her morning commute. If your goal is to reach all these various audiences, you will need specific communication products tailored differently for each.

Notice this isn't "dumbing it down"—that's an insult to the sophisticated, substantive experts who are both seeking and communicating evidence-based insights. This is about clarifying, simplifying, and leading with your insights while grounding them in evidence. Then make sure the data and details are available for everyone who wants to dig deeper.

Defining your audience is the first step to translating your research and then letting the conclusions from your analysis show the answers to critical questions.

The Pyramid Philosophy

There are a myriad ways to communicate your research: long reports, short briefs, interviews, blog posts, social media posts, presentations, and more. Your content may not be appropriate for all approaches, nor will every audience respond to each of them. It's useful to think of these different output types not as a box of options, but as a hierarchy. You are not necessarily pitting one audience against another or trading off sophistication for simplification. Rather, you are communicating your work in a multi-layered approach.

We like to think about communicating research using two mirroring pyramids, shown in the following graphic. On the one side is the *Complexity* pyramid. This is where we start this multilayered approach: At the bottom is the foundation of rigorously conducted research, typically a dense, technical report like a white paper or working paper. We then work our way up the pyramid—next comes the peer-reviewed journal article, which may strip out some of the working paper's denser analysis and exposition. Then comes the Congressional or expert testimony where your expertise is most important and is embedded within the written document. Further up the pyramid we find less technical and more accessible products such as fact sheets, briefings, blog posts, and media interviews; at the very top are social media posts.

We pair this *Complexity* pyramid with another pyramid that shows the size of the *Audience*. It's not surprising that only a few people are reading the working paper, and only a few more are reading the journal article. The audience for these products is small: The reader must make it through dozens of pages on methodology, literature review, and analysis across dozens or even hundreds of pages of formulas and tables before getting to the findings. Not many have the expertise to glean the insights that the author intends. But more people are reading briefs and fact sheets, and possibly many more are reading op-eds, commentaries, and blog posts. And possibly hundreds, maybe thousands, are reading that tweet or post on Facebook.

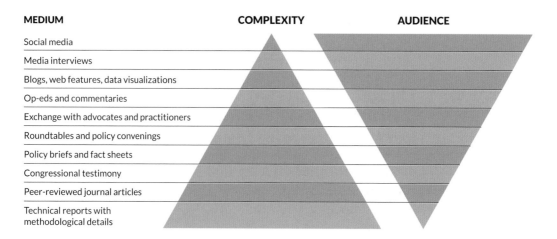

MEDIUM	COMPLEXITY	AUDIENCE
Social media		
Media interviews		
Blogs, web features, data visualizations		
Op-eds and commentaries		
Exchange with advocates and practitioners		
Roundtables and policy convenings		
Policy briefs and fact sheets		
Congressional testimony		
Peer-reviewed journal articles		
Technical reports with methodological details		

Here's the key: *Every product on the Complexity pyramid links to one below it, grounded in in-depth, sophisticated analysis.* Every blog post links to underlying evidence and a report. Every web feature includes the option to download a dataset or report. Every tweet finds its way back to a more in-depth analysis that provides evidence to support the claim made at each level of the pyramid. The data are available for the user who wants to dig deeper. Evidence is as deep—or deeper— than the question planted, and then answered in detail.

Be Your Own Translator

Many scholars and researchers consider public education their personal mission. Generous with their time, they go to great lengths to give people comprehensive explanations about their data and their research. Understandably, they get frustrated when their work is described inaccurately—by managers or reporters, panel moderators, or even colleagues. They assume the person didn't understand, missed the point, or doesn't care. They blame the *recipient* for their lack of sophistication or short attention span.

But that misunderstanding is, more often than not, the fault of the researcher who has not thought hard enough about how to explain his work. You may be an expert in education policy or international trade, but if you can't explain your work so your audience, reader, or reporter can understand it, it will go nowhere. That challenge is your burden to bear, so embrace it—and with a little extra effort, thought, and care, it will pay dividends.

We have limited recall. As developmental molecular biologist John Medina writes in his book *Brain Rules*, our brains can only hold about seven pieces of information for less than 30 seconds. Extending that memory requires consistently re-exposing yourself to the information. This doesn't seem unreasonable: Think back to the last presentation you attended or journal article you read. How much do you remember? Perhaps two or three takeaways stuck with you—if the presentation was very well done or the article was clearly written. Perhaps not even that many.

Never go into a discussion without first articulating exactly the two or three points you want your reader or listener to remember. Force yourself to go through the clichéd-but-valuable mental exercise of summarizing or explaining your research to your parents, your neighbor, your teenager, or another interested nonexpert.

Here are some other questions to help you formulate your takeaways:

- What are the two or three most interesting findings from your research?
- What surprised you?
- Which statistics, percentages, or facts are particularly noteworthy?
- What are the policy implications of your research?
- What challenges did you face while conducting the research?
- Why is your research so important?

Put yourself directly in the role of your user. If you were writing the article for the *New York Times*, how would you write the headline? What would be your lead paragraph? How would you be quoted? What would be your tweet?

By putting yourself in the position of the reporter, you can be more attuned to what it is they need from your research and what they need from your explanation. How can your work help them make discoveries, find insights, and solve problems? Put another way, this is *empathy*. In his effort to improve communication skills for scientists, Alan Alda, the actor-turned-staunch defender of science, says, "Effective science communication happens when we listen and connect. It happens when we use empathy. Communication is headed for success when we pay more attention to what the other person is understanding rather than focusing solely on what we want to say."

Wrapping It in a Personal Story

Many researchers—especially those who focus on quantitative analysis—fail to recognize the importance of connecting with the reader or audience on an emotional level. One way to do so is through stories. Stories seem trivial to many researchers, who fear that by sharing a personal anecdote, they risk undermining the subtlety, nuance, and details of the data or statistical analysis. But humans are wired to relate to and remember stories, not statistics, which is why the neurobiology of storytelling is now being applied to both business and academia. Some experts estimate that people retain information when it is weaved into narratives over *22 times better* than facts alone. Some even speculate that stories can persuade people to *change their minds*, becoming more empathetic, compassionate, and open. Stories are not the *entirety* of your communication strategy, of course; rather, they should be used to help *illustrate* your work, grounding your research in the human experience and demonstrating why your research is relevant to your audience.

A story will help illuminate this point. A colleague wanted to practice her presentation before heading off to give a keynote address at an academic conference. She and her research team had explored the experience families around Denver, Colorado, were having with state social service offices. We gathered together and she started her presentation by laying out the agenda, discussing the previous literature, and diving into the data and details, before ultimately delivering the policy conclusions. It was a standard academic presentation following the standard approach. When she finished, we provided her with some basic feedback, for example, around some of the dense, hard-to-read slides. What happened next was the key to the afternoon. In the discussion that followed, the research team described some of the interviews they had conducted with families in Denver: a couple who had difficulty completing application forms; a single mom who struggled to get her kids to school and had to take three buses downtown to apply for her benefits. These stories drew us all in—no data, no statistics, just stories about people struggling to support themselves and their families. It powerfully illustrated why research matters—and why we must evaluate and improve programs so they can serve people better. Ultimately, the researcher replaced a portion of her presentation with these stories to demonstrate how her research is relevant to the real world.

There are countless examples of the power of story and, be it through your speaking or your writing, stories can have a profound effect. You need not use stories as the central focus of your work, nor must your story give a universal lesson or truth, but you can and should use them to make your work memorable. Ground your evidence in the lived experience of communities you care about. Consider telling stories about challenges you had conducting the research, or why you were motivated to conduct the research, or interesting findings you uncovered—or better yet, from real people in their own words. Your stories will connect you to your audience.

Writing Your Broader Narrative

Once you've gotten into the practice of reducing complexity, honing your insights, and using a story to demonstrate why your research matters, it's time to think about your broader narrative. Go beyond one or two publications to explain more broadly why your research matters. Why do you do what you do? What questions are you asking? What impact do you want your work to have? Are you using language that is inclusive, and are you providing historical and societal context for problems people are facing? The *Complexity* pyramid does not include *all* potential outputs, and it is often the case that thinking more broadly across multiple platforms and publications can help your work have an even greater impact.

Three examples nicely illustrate the point:

1. Matthew Desmond joined Harvard University after earning his PhD in sociology from the University of Wisconsin at Madison.

After conducting research on race, urban poverty, and housing, publishing in numerous peer-reviewed journals and writing various columns in the *New York Times*, Desmond published his best-selling book *Evicted: Poverty and Profit in the American City*. In it, he follows eight families in Milwaukee, Wisconsin, as they struggle with poverty and housing challenges. He successfully shows the role that eviction plays in trapping families in poverty with one powerful story after another, all grounded in evidence. With the support of different funders, Desmond then founded the Eviction Lab at Princeton University, which makes nationwide eviction data available and accessible to a wider audience.

2. Kathryn Edin, a sociologist currently at Princeton University, used the power of story to show the impossibility of living on two dollars a day. After more than 20 years conducting sociological research on poverty, parenting, and taxes, Edin teamed up with another professor, Luke Shaefer from the University of Michigan, to examine survey data on people with extremely low incomes. Edin and Shaefer published their work in peer-reviewed journals and edited volumes. In their 2016 book, *$2.00 a Day: Living on Almost Nothing in America*, Edin and Shaefer combined their quantitative data analysis with on-the-ground interviews with people struggling with exceptionally low incomes.

3. Raj Chetty is an economist at Stanford University. Early in his career, Chetty's research focused on taxes and labor markets, appearing in some of the top journals in the field. Around 2013, Chetty was examining patterns in earnings and income mobility (the propensity to move around in the earnings or income distribution) over time, between generations, and within specific geographic areas, using administrative data from the Internal Revenue Service and the Social Security Administration. Chetty would later found a collaborative project and website, the Equality of Opportunity Project, with researchers from Brown University and Harvard University, among others, to help provide data and analysis to a broader audience.

You don't necessarily need a team of researchers and an advance for a best-selling book to refine your stories and hone your narrative. Any researcher can do this by weaving her work together to form a thesis about why problems exist and how to overcome them.

Use Every Tool to Communicate Your Insights

Once you've articulated your insights, narrative, and stories, start using them everywhere. All the time. Repeat them over and over and over, until you're sick of them. And then repeat them some more. Your insights should lead the summary of your report and your blog post. They should be flagged in your media interviews and quoted by reporters. They should show up in your tweets. In time, they should become associated with your identity as a scholar—your personal brand. Though many researchers will scoff at the term *personal brand*, this is what you are doing when you are asking others to read, listen, and embrace your work. You are "selling" them on your ideas.

Remember that not every person will read or see every product in your research pyramid. Embracing your insights will help you reach more people. And reaching more people is not about becoming famous or being quoted in the *New York Times*. It may not even directly lead to promotions or tenure. But reaching more people may lead you to new collaborators, new funders, or new data, which can lead to these other milestones. Taking the time to build your own strategic communication plan can ultimately lead to big rewards, not just personally, but also in the area in which you study.

Wrapping Up

We have developed this book to help you—the researcher, the analyst, the thought leader, the scholar—do a better job communicating your work. You may not have a communications department to lean on, to help you get your content out in the world. You may need to do this on your own. But it doesn't need to be painful, and it doesn't have to be difficult. With a few simple lessons on how to make better graphs, give better presentations, write better blog posts, and give better interviews, you can help get your research in the hands of people who can use it.

The lessons in this book are intended to help you design your own communications strategy, and that strategy begins by recognizing the importance of your work and the different channels available to you to reach your audiences.

Case Study: *Creating a range of products to reach different audiences*

In 2018, a team of researchers in the Urban Institute's Metropolitan Housing and Communities Policy Center was preparing for the release of a report they knew would make a big splash. Urban researchers have studied housing discrimination for years, examining its effects on people of color, people with disabilities, families with children, same-sex couples, and transgender people. Now they were adding another group to that list: housing voucher holders.

In their 2018 pilot study, the team presented findings from the largest, most comprehensive test of housing discrimination, providing data on housing voucher acceptance among landlords. The team looked at landlords' acceptance of housing vouchers in Los Angeles, California; Fort Worth, Texas; Philadelphia, Pennsylvania; Washington, DC; and Newark, New Jersey, and found that landlords consistently rejected voucher holders, limiting their access to decent housing in good neighborhoods.

The team's findings were big news in the housing world, but different audiences needed different information. Local media wanted more details about the results in their specific areas, federal policymakers wanted to know about broader implications for the Housing Choice Voucher Program, and other researchers wanted to know about the methodology behind their study.

The research team worked with Urban's communications staff to figure out which products and messages were best suited for which audiences. In addition to the main research report, they developed several products:

1. An expanded abstract and executive summary with key findings and takeaways for policymakers.
2. Five fact sheets with detailed information on each of the five cities.
3. A 700-word blog post about the overall findings and policy implications for a national audience.
4. Targeted emails sent to a range of stakeholders.
5. Media pitches tailored to local and national outlets.
6. A PowerPoint slide deck that included more detailed methodological information for other researchers.

After the initial release, the research team continued looking for other opportunities where they could share their work and further cement themselves as experts in the housing discrimination field. In the months after the report's release, they published two more blog posts for Urban's main blog, *Urban Wire*, and the *Urban-Greater DC* website about the Los Angeles and DC-specific results; wrote an op-ed for a Texas news outlet; discussed their findings with congressional staff; and included the study results in testimony to the House Subcommittee on Transportation, Housing and Urban Development, and related agencies.

The team's efforts paid off. The report was widely cited in national and local media. The Department of Housing and Urban Development, which funded the study, launched a listening tour with landlords and local stakeholders around the country because of the research. And the Los Angeles County Board of Supervisors moved to outlaw discrimination against housing voucher holders, citing the Urban report as a key driver behind their effort.

(continued)

The Urban research team understood that a lengthy and complex report wasn't the best way to reach all audiences. They created shorter, more accessible products and tailored their messaging and focus to different groups who could take the results of the research and make meaningful change.

"We put all these products out there so they would make sense to different audiences in different ways," says Martha Galvez, a principal research associate who worked on the project. "This range of products gave us a lot of tools to be able to get to people where they are."

chapter two

Developing an Audience Outreach Strategy

Amy Elsbree and Amy Peake

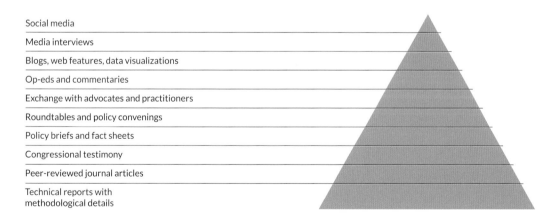

Social media

Media interviews

Blogs, web features, data visualizations

Op-eds and commentaries

Exchange with advocates and practitioners

Roundtables and policy convenings

Policy briefs and fact sheets

Congressional testimony

Peer-reviewed journal articles

Technical reports with
methodological details

The first step in developing a communication strategy for your work is to identify your audience. Depending on your goals, your target audience can range from a handful of academic experts to policymakers to interested members of the public. The most successful outreach campaigns are deliberate about who they are trying to reach and how they will reach them.

Communicating directly with your audience and other stakeholders can help get your work in the right hands and elevate your profile. You may not be seeking fame and fortune, but raising your profile can help you connect with new colleagues, new research opportunities, new funders, and new data sources. By effectively identifying and purposefully communicating with the most relevant groups, you help ensure that the right people can see and know how to act on your research, going beyond hoping they happen to catch the mention of the research in the news or glance at social media at the right time. Ultimately, this method of communication—purposeful, direct personal outreach—helps strengthen your relationships so you and your audiences can help influence policy and effect change.

Later chapters dive into tactics for using communications platforms that can help you reach your audience through media relations, social media, blogging, data visualizations, and other means. Using these other communications platforms not only helps you reach the public, thought leaders, and influencers, but also helps build your credibility and your reputation, and it helps facilitate future conversations with policymakers.

In this chapter, we help you define the *who* of your audience (hint: it's not *everyone*). We will especially focus on how to do direct outreach to the policymaker audience, which in many cases is the primary target for policy recommendations.

Identifying Your Audience

When we ask researchers who they are trying to reach with their research, we hear a common response: "*Everyone. Everyone* will be interested. *Everyone* will want to see the results. If I reach *everyone*, then *everyone* will include important people, and my recommendations will be put into action."

But that's just not how outreach and communications work. People have different interests, different priorities, and different levels of understanding. Think about what you expect your colleagues or managers to do with your work compared with an audience of practitioners or policymakers. One audience may need a nuanced, thorough analysis of the data and methods; another may need the punchline and the most important, bottom-line numbers or facts. Your work will be stronger and your impact will be wider if you can reach people with diverse backgrounds.

Successfully reaching an audience first requires you to conceptualize your audience. Trying to reach *everyone* will often result in reaching no one. To begin, ask yourself four broad sets of questions:

1. **What is your goal?** Do you want to share your research results? Are you looking for collaborators, more data, more funding? Are you looking to change ideas or policies?

2. **Who can help you meet your goals?** Which people have influence on those who hold the levers, and who are the people driving change in the community on these issues?

3. **Which policymakers or decisionmakers hold the levers for the government program or issue you are researching?** At what level of government—local, state, federal—will your work be most useful and applicable? What nonprofits, practitioners, or private-sector companies will find your work valuable?

4. **Where is your access most likely to be successful?** Which researchers, organizations, or policymakers will most likely help you reach your goals, and in turn help your audience reach their goals?

Answering a few initial questions about the type of people you want to reach will help you focus on what you want people to do with your research and refine your target audience. With these goals in mind, it's time to target your specific audience—and remember, not all audiences are the same. There are a multitude of different people that you should consider, and we have placed them into seven main groups:

1. **Academic and research organizations.** You may be focused on information- or data-sharing, or you may be interested in moving your field ahead technically or theoretically. Consider universities and colleges, research associations, and data organizations that are doing similar work or working in the same area as you.

2. **Nonprofit organizations.** What organizations work in the same area as your research and might benefit from the results and recommendations? Consider advocacy groups, service providers, charities, activists, membership organizations, and community stakeholders. Be sure you have included people with lived experience who could be represented by community or advocacy organizations.

3. **Funders.** You may need financial support to continue or expand your research, or funders and other philanthropic organizations may be able to use your research in their own work. See if you can identify specific funders or organizations working in your area.

4. **Federal agency and executive branch employees.** The U.S. federal government employs more than 2 million full-time workers. Simply targeting the federal government is almost like targeting *everyone*. Are specific agencies, groups, or committees especially relevant? Also consider independent government agencies.

5. **Members of the federal legislative branch.** The U.S. Congress is made up of 435 members of the House of Representatives and 100 senators. There are 650 members of Parliament in the United Kingdom and 790 seats in the Parliament of India. And these large organizations are not limited to elected members. In the United States, congressional staffers work directly for each member of Congress in Washington, DC, and the member's home district or state. There are also highly specialized policy staffs in congressional committees and caucuses, along with researchers at the Library of Congress, Congressional Budget Office, and Government Accountability Office. How can your research help or provide legislators with evidence for a policy or program?

6. **State and local elected and program officials.** Thomas P. "Tip" O'Neill, Jr., was Speaker of the House of Representatives from 1977 to 1987 and is commonly associated with the phrase, "All politics is local." It may not be a far cry to also say, "all *policy* is local." The results of your research may be best used and implemented by local decision- and policymakers. Consider not only specific local elected leaders but large associations like the National Governors Association or the National League of Cities

(both in the United States). You may also consider staff members of elected officials, program directors, and practitioners.

7. **Private sector.** Is your work applicable to private-sector entities such as businesses and consultants? Perhaps certain private-sector organizations can use your work in their own projects— and others may be willing to fund your work.

As you work through these groups, use the checklist at the end of this chapter to help guide your thinking (and download an editable copy on the book's website, https://www.urban.org/Elevatethe-DebateBook). This checklist breaks down our seven groups in more detail to help spur your thinking about the types of organizations that might be eager to hear about your work.

Visualizing (and Finding) Your Audience

One way to figure out which audience would be receptive to your research is to imagine if you had that role. If you were a mayor, member of Congress, or CEO, what could you do with this research? Write a law? Set up a new program? Help fund further research?

Imagine yourself as the mayor: Your challenges include making sure potholes are filled, the public is safe from harm, and your city is attracting jobs and businesses. As mayor, what actions could you take on the research insight? Start a program? A task force? Or is the mayor not the right person for this specific work? Do a little online research to match what you imagined against reality. Does your mayor have the authority or jurisdiction to make a change based on your insight? Is she interested in this as part of her political agenda? If she's not, might the vice-mayor or another council member be interested?

Narrow Your Focus

Don't try to do too much. It's better to find a smaller group of people who will be keenly interested in your work than a wider group that may gloss over it. You'll want to assess the best chances you have to reach the key audience members and use that to narrow your focus.

Here, we can rely on the business concept of return on investment, or ROI. In this case, the investment is the time you spend having conversations with policymakers; if you spend too much time on outreach, you'll lose the time to develop new evidence and add to the research base. Finding the right balance between communications and research is up to you.

One of Urban's research teams who examines family savings and their impact on local governments has struck a good balance between conducting the research and connecting with their target audience. When doing new research, this team plans ahead and asks the communication team to help develop fact sheets highlighting the research. Research team create visualizations that cities can use to find data, making it easier to facilitate conversations directly with policymakers who are eager to get quickly to the point of the research.

But most important, these researchers are also thoughtful about saying yes to webinars and meetings where the ROI will be high. They attend webinars and convenings hosted by the National League of Cities, where local government leaders gather. These local leaders are interested in the research topic already and are often seen as capable and trusted influencers among their peers. By delivering their research directly into the hands of local officials who are already interested in sharing the information, the research team is leveraging specific opportunities to reach their intended audience.

Defining "Policymakers"

"Policymakers" is a broad term that could mean federal, state, or local government officials. It could mean elected officials or appointed officials such as a cabinet secretary or government agency head. It could also mean staff members who work closely with these officials, either directly or on committees or working groups. These staffers might, in fact, be your best vehicle to get your research into the hands of the policymakers.

In Practice: Finding and Building an Audience for Urban's Education Policy Research

---

When Urban launched an education-policy team in early 2018, we worked closely with the lead researchers to understand the audiences who could act on insights from education policy research.

There is a large constituency for education-policy insights: local school boards, state elected officials, parents, teachers, advocates for kids, federal agencies, and Congress, not to mention the students themselves! Basically, *everyone* could have an interest in education policy. But our researchers couldn't reach *everyone*. Instead, we thought about the types of people most receptive and able to most easily and quickly put the research into action.

In anticipating how each audience type could put the research into practice, the research team focused on three primary groups. First, they decided to connect with congressional staffers regarding higher education issues, especially student loan policy. This makes sense: Congress has legislative authority and is actively debating these issues. Second, because of the wide array of datasets and analyses to conduct on education policy, the team personally connected with academic researchers to begin harnessing education data sources. Third, the research team regularly participates in meetings and briefings with nonprofit organizations who are trusted sources for parents, students, teachers, and others looking for information about education policy. Working with these groups helps the education researchers reach a broader audience without trying to directly contact *everyone* around the country interested in education policy.

We encourage researchers to try to think about policymakers in specific categories, and we have developed the following diagram to help them organize their efforts. Along the top of the diagram, we consider the three levels of government in the United States: federal, state, and local. We also include associations that span all three levels; for example, the National Governors Association and the National League of Cities are channels to governors and mayors.

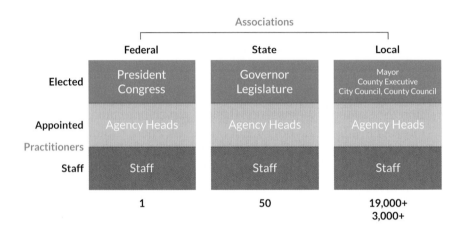

Along the left side of the diagram, we differentiate between elected and appointed officials and the staff members for various offices. Elected officials include the president and members of Congress; governors and legislatures; and mayors, county executives, and maybe even school board members. Elected officials often have a vested interest in meeting with you, particularly if you're a constituent. Mayors, county supervisors, members of Congress, and others might hold office hours or have staff that can help you schedule a short meeting. Most elected officials also have public or published email addresses where you can directly contact the official—or at least a member of their staff.

Notably, we introduce "practitioners" here, a broad term we use to capture those officials, staff, and agency leaders who are running programs, delivering services, and making decisions daily that shape how a policy is carried out. Don't underestimate the impact you can have by communicating directly with these important players. These individuals often understand specific policies and programs at an even deeper level than elected officials. These practitioners—often a combination of high-level staff and some appointed officials—may be able to institute change themselves or convince the higher-ups to make a change.

The diagram also lists the size of the audience in each of these groups. There is only one federal government, but there are 50 states, more than 3,000 counties, and more than 19,000 cities, towns, boroughs, and townships in the United States. Let's say you have an important insight or policy recommendation about the child welfare system. Although your first instinct might be to jump on the next plane to Washington, DC and talk with the congressional committee that handles the federal child-welfare law, you might have more impact by reaching out to county leaders who have the "levers" to effect change more quickly in their communities.

As an example, researchers in the Housing Finance Policy Center at Urban have briefed the federal secretary of Housing and Urban Development (HUD) and have had calls with local housing boards and city officials (see the *Case Study* at the end of this chapter). Most of the day-to-day emails and outreach, however, are directly to HUD staffers or executive directors of local housing authorities.

Finding Contact Information for Policymakers

Finding contact information for policymakers is easier than you might think. Check official sources like your secretary of state's website (or a phone directory if your area has them) for officials' names and contact information. It might be tempting to pick the name at the top of the list or organization chart, but take the time to find a title of someone who might have a job that connects directly to your research area. We often connect directly with state offices, but we don't always start with the head of the state agency. Instead we sometimes work with the chiefs of staff or policy or research directors. These practitioners are already in the weeds and might be most up to speed on the field generally and open to new research or insights.

Working with Networks and Associations

It can be a big job to reach the large pool of state or local leaders and policymakers. This is why associations can be helpful tools. In any issue area or an area "vertical" of government issues, you will find an organization that brings together like officials—for example, the American Public Transportation Association for bus and transit operators and managers; the National Association of City and County Health Officials; or the National School Boards Association.

Any membership or professional association can become an aggregator of information and research. By developing a relationship with staff and finding out how to share your content with them, you can reach their membership across the country through their official communications channels. Because the association is a trusted source of information, their emails will get opened, articles will get read, and webinars and events attended.

Also think about the local or state chapters of national associations. Most states, for example, have a municipal league for city governments, like the Colorado Municipal League or the County Welfare Directors Association of California. Starting with someone local provides the opportunity to meet face to face with staff and to further refine your messages before going national.

Conceptualizing Your Audience to Guide Your Outreach

Building a relationship with your audience that yields tangible impact for your work happens over time. You need to play the long game, building up visibility for your expertise and your recommendations. At Urban, we offer our researchers a consistent way to conceptualize and measure audience engagement through a stakeholder-mapping graph (see below/next page).

The horizontal axis in this diagram represents the *strength* of your relationship with your audience. On the left side are groups or individuals with whom your relationship may be weak or even non-existent. On the right are those with whom you are in regular contact, who use and appreciate your work, and who you can count on to share your work with a wider network.

Along the vertical axis, we plot the *influence* of the individual or group. Can they help you reach major newspapers or websites? Might they connect you with specific policymakers, organizations, or staff? Or perhaps they can pull certain policy levers themselves?

CONCEPTUALIZING YOUR AUDIENCE

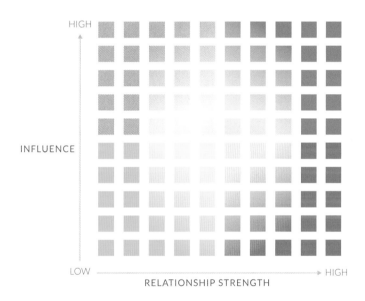

INFLUENCERS

Inform with relevant, timely, useful information

Direct email, events, and retail engagement

KEY STAKEHOLDERS

Keep informed with regular, personal contact; enlist strategically

Personal email, speaker requests, and in-person engagement

FAN CLUB

Keep informed and engaged; enlist periodically

Newsletters, social media, and events

OTHERS

Keep Informed

Newsletters and social media

Let's define the four groups in this space, starting in the top left:

Influencers. Those in the gray squares have influence, but they don't know you well, if at all. These might be thought leaders, authors, and other researchers who could help circulate your work to a wider audience and perhaps even put your work into practice. The influencers group likely contains the policymakers, practitioners, and their staffs that can put your research into action. The more you can ultimately connect with this group, the higher the likelihood your message will spread and have the impact you want.

We encourage our experts to fully understand the context and interests of an influencer. If we have a large data tool, for example, that includes information on supporting work for people who access public assistance, we will send an email to influencers who run anti-hunger programs that is slightly different than our email to practitioners who implement workforce training programs. Although both types of influencers might be interested in the data tool, they start with different priorities and knowledge base.

You can also rely on social media, blogs, news media, and other communications to introduce yourself to influencers (see Chapters 5, 6, and 7). If, however, you want to ensure influencers hear what you have to say, directly engaging with them is a good approach. Plus, it allows you to highly tailor and customize your message to make it relevant for the influencer.

Key stakeholders. Those in the blue squares, on the top right, are both influential *and* know you and your work. These friends, current and former colleagues, partners, funders, and collaborators open your emails, help spread your message across social media, share your newsletters, recommend you as an expert to a journalist, and might even seek you out for your insights.

Our researchers affectionately call these key stakeholders their "blues" (which also happens to be Urban's primary logo color, so it's easy for us all to remember). What does it take to maintain a good relationship with a blue? Time and effort. Perhaps after your report is published, you send a thoughtful personal note with a thank you to outside colleagues who read early drafts of your research. You might give a special call to someone who works at an organization focused on a similar issue, adding a thank you for their dedication and an overview of how the research relates to their mission. If you host an event or conference session, you might invite your blue friends to also present their work. This gives them the opportunity to share their work, even in cases where it doesn't agree with yours.

Checking in with your key stakeholders early and often is important to build these relationships. Once you have a strong relationship, you should have developed a good understanding of your blues and the things that are relevant to their workplaces. You want to grow the blue area of this diagram, so you are connected with people who trust you and look to you for insight and recommendations.

Understanding these friends (your key stakeholders) and how to help them achieve their goals is good practice for understanding how to connect your work to the *Influencers* group, which is the group that you most want to reach.

Fan club. Those in the pink squares, on the bottom right, know you well, appreciate your work, and follow you closely, but they may not currently have positions of influence. These are people who follow you on social media, read your or your organization's newsletter, and attend similar events and conferences.

Your fans are an important part of your network. They can boost your credibility and help get the word out about your insights—think of them as your personal brand ambassadors. Make sure to keep them posted on what your insights are and what is important to you. When the time is right, don't be afraid to ask if they know anyone that might be interested in your work. They might retweet you on Twitter or forward your emails. Although you might reach them with your newsletter or online, they are probably not the right people to spend many hours preparing for a direct, in-person stakeholder outreach style conversation about how to put your research into practice.

Others. Those yellow squares in the bottom-left part don't know you and can't necessarily directly affect policy or act on your insights.

They don't really engage with your work and are not people who are going to bring it to the attention of other stakeholders, nor are they going to act upon it themselves. They might read about your work on social media or if you are mentioned in a news article. They do not have any influence in your content area, and although they might be part of a wider audience whose hearts and minds you are trying to change, spending lots of time trying to reach this audience using direct stakeholder outreach is not the most practical approach given limited time and resources.

In Practice: Audience Advisory Groups

At Urban, some of our researchers have set up advisory groups of practitioners, advocates, and associations that are periodically updated on the research while it is in process. Not only are these advisors helpful in making the research stronger, they will often help share research projects once they are completed with their own networks.

Sometimes, informal conversations work well too: When one of our research teams was debating between a short video or an infographic, we reached out to our blues for their opinion and heard back a preference for copyable text. We went with an infographic and a report. Not only did we want to make sure our research reached our audience, we wanted to make sure it was easy for them to understand and act on.

In-Person Outreach: Presenting Your Key Findings

Once you've identified your key audience, it's time to think concretely about how to present your insights and recommendations to that audience. Elected officials, appointed officials, and practitioners, for example, are seeking different levels of detail, as we've outlined in the diagram on the next page. Elected officials, for example, are likely interested in the fact, statistic, or story that they can quickly and easily grasp to communicate with their colleagues and constituents. Practitioners, by contrast, may want the full research paper and details of the methodology to more fully understand the approach and implications of your work.

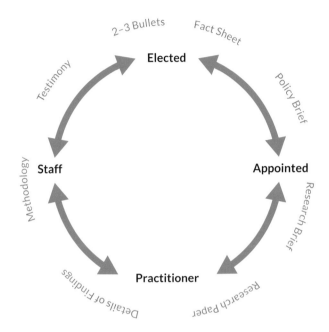

For meetings or briefings with elected officials and senior managers, one-pagers with bullets and clear, concise message points are often effective tools. Consider creating more visual content for one-pagers by including graphs, illustrations, or photographs that match your longer report or website (see Chapter 4).

If you are meeting with practitioners or staff for senior officials, they will likely be more interested in the research brief or even a longer study. In some cases, they might be interested in understanding the underlying methodology or data. When you are working with staff, practitioners, and junior officials, you need to ensure that your recommendations are realistic. Walking in the door to propose a multimillion-dollar program increase won't earn you any credibility with a practitioner whose reality is having to serve more people with fewer resources. Instead, meet them where they are; perhaps pull out a smaller key point or a takeaway that could be implemented and accomplished. Build your trust and credibility over time by finding what is relevant to practitioners and helping them work smarter.

When you speak with elected officials, their staffs, and certain thought leaders, it's important that you connect your work and insights to their stated priorities. Frame your work in terms of solutions and the impact they will have on people's lives. Having been elected by the community, officials want to frame their decisions in larger terms: "This means more families get fed," "This means our streets are safer," and "This means we will attract more investment from businesses in our community." Your research and recommendations will resonate and be more actionable if you can help the officials by speaking their language and show how your work helps them accomplish what they've set out to do.

Mix and Match Your Communications Practices

Developing an audience-outreach strategy is a two-step process: Figure out *who* and *how*. In this chapter, we have focused on helping you identify the *who*—those thought leaders, decisionmakers, and policymakers you can identify who will generate the greatest ROI to your research and what you need to think about when connecting directly to those target audiences.

The next several chapters will help you identify the *how*. Although directly engaging with a specific audience can get your message directly into the hands of the policymakers you would like to reach, you should mix and match communications methods to create a full outreach plan (Chapter 8). Think about how a media story might soften the ground and raise awareness of your work before you deliver testimony or speak to an elected official (Chapter 6). Consider whether engaging on a social media platform like Twitter or

Facebook could reach an elected official or CEO of a company just as well (or better) than a meeting or phone call that can be hard to get (Chapter 7). An effective data visualization might draw in a policy-maker's staffer who is trying to understand an issue deeper, resulting in a phone call or a conversation (Chapter 3). An updated web presence through social media and blogging—summarizing your research and credentials, for example—will bolster your reputation and credibility before you walk in the door to meet with an elected official (Chapter 5).

These plans take time and effort. Your work will not immediately appear on the front page of the *New York Times* because you tweeted to your favorite reporter. You won't necessarily be asked to testify because you spoke to your city council member. But you can get there. By carefully considering your approach and your audience, you can help communicate your findings to your desired audience, build trust, and achieve your goals—be it new coverage, new collaborators, more funding, or policy impact.

Key Takeaways

- Identify your audience. The most effective outreach campaigns are deliberate about who they are trying to reach and how they will reach them.
- Narrow your focus. Trying to reach everyone often results in reaching no one. It's better to find a smaller group of people who are keenly interested in your work than a wider group that may gloss over it.
- Play the long game. Building a relationship with your audience happens over time. Take the time to understand where your audience members are in their engagement and influence, and build from there.
- Meet your audience where they are. Build your trust and credibility by finding what is relevant to them and giving them the level of detail (or lack of detail) they need.

Audience and List Brainstorming

Building an audience list can include thinking through already established contacts and stakeholders. Consider recently attended conferences, email newsletters, project stakeholders, focus groups for a project, advocates who reached out, or practitioners you worked with. Try to connect with a diverse mix of people from various backgrounds and also consider people with lived experience.

Here are a few places—admittedly U.S.-focused—to think through to help in audience brainstorming:

Academic and Research Organizations
- ❑ Researchers at think tanks (e.g., Urban Institute, Pew Research Center, RAND Corporation, Brookings Institution)
- ❑ Staff or members of research associations (e.g., National Association for Welfare Research and Statistics)
- ❑ Scholars and academics
- ❑ Data organizations (e.g., NORC at the University of Chicago, Census Bureau)

Nonprofit Organizations
- ❑ Membership organizations (e.g., Economic Analysis and Research Network, US Chamber of Commerce, American Medical Association)
- ❑ Advocacy groups (e.g., National Low Income Housing Coalition, National Women's Law Center, AARP)
- ❑ Civil rights organizations (e.g., UnidosUS, Human Rights Campaign, Leadership Conference on Civil and Human Rights)
- ❑ Community stakeholders (e.g., local organizations for any places named in your project)
- ❑ Service providers (e.g., United Way, community health centers, food banks)

- ❏ Community activists, grassroots organizations, and advocates for populations (e.g., MomsRising, National Fair Housing Alliance, National Head Start Association, Children's Defense Fund)
- ❏ Charities and philanthropy (e.g., Catholic Charities, Salvation Army, Red Cross)

Federal Government and Executive Branch
- ❏ Appointees, policymakers, or grantmakers at cabinet-level departments (e.g., US Departments of Housing and Urban Development, Health and Human Services, Agriculture, Education, Labor, and Justice)
- ❏ Appointees or policymakers at independent agencies (e.g., US Interagency Council on Homelessness, Consumer Financial Protection Bureau, Federal Housing Finance Agency)
- ❏ White House staffers or appointees (e.g., Council of Economic Advisers, Office of Management and Budget, Domestic Policy Council, Office of the Vice President)
- ❏ White House initiatives or cabinet-level initiatives (e.g., White House Initiative on Educational Excellence for Hispanics, White House Task Force on Puerto Rico, Office of Intergovernmental Affairs, Office for Civil Rights)

Funders
- ❏ Program officers of funding organizations for this project and past projects (e.g., Annie E. Casey Foundation, Ford Foundation, W. K. Kellogg Foundation)
- ❏ Philanthropic community organizations (e.g., East Bay Community Foundation)
- ❏ Entrepreneurs (e.g., Bill & Melinda Gates Foundation, Chan Zuckerberg Initiative)

Legislative Body
- ❏ Staffers who work in senators' or representatives' offices
- ❏ Staffers who work for a congressional committee (e.g., Joint Committee on Taxation; Senate Committee on Health, Education, Labor and Pensions; House Ways and Means Committee)

- ❏ Staffers who work for congressional caucuses (e.g., Congressional LGBT Equality Caucus, Congressional Asian Pacific American Caucus, House Hunger Caucus)
- ❏ Researchers at the Library of Congress, Congressional Budget Office, or Government Accountability Office

State and Local Elected and Program Officials

- ❏ Associations of elected officials or civil servants (e.g., National Governors Association, National League of Cities)
- ❏ Elected officials (e.g., mayors, governors, county supervisors)
- ❏ Staff to elected officials (e.g., a mayor's chief of staff, a city manager, or a county administrator)
- ❏ Program directors or practitioners (e.g., program officers at a public housing authority, a county welfare director)

Private Sector

- ❏ Consultants and consulting firms (e.g., Accenture, Boston Consulting Group, Deloitte)
- ❏ Businesses and startups (e.g., Airbnb, Lyft)

Your Personal Audience

- ❏ Colleagues in your department or division
- ❏ Colleagues in other departments, divisions, organizations, or universities
- ❏ Trustees or board of directors
- ❏ Social media networks (e.g., Facebook, LinkedIn, Twitter)
- ❏ Friends and other personal relationships

Case Study: *Targeting your outreach efforts to different audiences*

One of the main goals of Urban Institute's Housing Finance Policy Center (HFPC) is to give a high-level audience of decisionmakers new data and evidence to help them make better-informed policies about housing finance. They have spent time and effort building out ways to reach their various audiences using different platforms and techniques.

Some of the audiences they connect with regularly include federal government analysts and administrators, congressional and administration staff, practitioners, funders, and analysts. HFPC reaches these audiences through methods ranging from direct emails to regularly scheduled conference calls. Each method is deliberate for the audience they are trying to reach.

One of the team's vice presidents maintains a tailored email list of funders and other primary stakeholders. She reaches out to people on this list with direct, personal emails when new Urban research is particularly relevant to their or their organization's needs and interests. The team's communications director maintains a broader list of more than 200 associates, contacts, decisionmakers, and media members who receive more regular updates of the center's work.

Each month, HFPC researchers publish a chartbook with more than 60 tables, charts, and graphs about housing finance. Much of this information is available in public data, but the research team has distilled it in a simple, understandable way. With help from their communications director, the researchers hold a quarterly call with their most highly engaged audience (their "blues" from Chapter 2) including staffers from the Consumer Financial Protection Bureau, the Department of Housing and

(continued)

Urban Development, county housing authorities, Senate staffers, and many analysts.

Social media is also an effective method the team uses to capitalize on the reputation of an HFPC vice president. When this highly respected researcher joined the Urban Institute, she was not regularly reaching out to a wide range of decisionmakers. HFPC's communications director set up Twitter and LinkedIn pages, which she now uses to highlight relevant research and blog posts with short, digestible posts. The vice president now has over 4,000 followers on Twitter and 2,600 connections on LinkedIn, including senate staffers, U.S. Treasury and Consumer Financial Protection Bureau officials, association and foundation leaders, and funders.

Urban's housing finance team's focus on using different communications methods to connect with various decisionmaker and influencer audiences has paid off. Their research is widely cited in academic journals as well as popular media, researchers are regularly invited to testify on Capitol Hill, and they often meet with staff and heads of different federal agencies. By creating different outreach methods and effectively tailoring those methods to their audiences, these researchers have helped their work reach more people and have a direct impact on public policy.

chapter three

An Introduction to Visualizing Your Research

Jonathan Schwabish

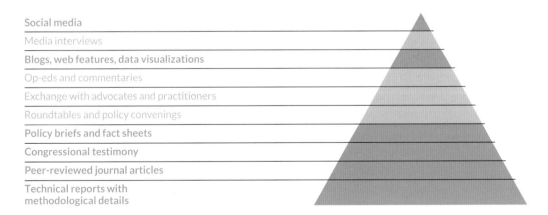

Social media

Media interviews

Blogs, web features, data visualizations

Op-eds and commentaries

Exchange with advocates and practitioners

Roundtables and policy convenings

Policy briefs and fact sheets

Congressional testimony

Peer-reviewed journal articles

Technical reports with
methodological details

Now that you have an idea of your overall approach and the audience (or audiences) you want to reach, you can start thinking about the different visual, text, media, and social media outlets available to disseminate your work. In this chapter, we start with improving how you visualize your data. Graphs, charts, and diagrams have long been part of the analyst's toolbox, but only more recently has interest in better ways to visualize data grown.

It may come as no surprise that many scholars, researchers, and analysts leave the visual component of their communication efforts to the last minute. Yes, many make graphs and visuals as they learn about their data and analysis, but when it comes time to present those findings in a presentation or written report, the visuals are often thrown together without carefully considering the needs of the audience or readers, such as their levels of expertise with the content or even the graph type.

In this chapter, I provide you with the fundamentals to visualize your data better and more effectively. I show you how to visually present your analysis so that your readers can spend their time focusing on your content and less time trying to decipher what they're looking at.

As you work with your data, don't leave the visualization process to the last minute. First, consider whether you need a graph at all: many graphs are added to reports because the author believes the text simply needs a visual. Whatever you create, it should have a purpose. It should further the argument you are making or the story you are telling. You wouldn't include unnecessary or extraneous variables in your regression models, nor would you include unnecessary words in your written text, so take the same approach with your data visualizations. Second, remember that your reader may be seeing your content for the first time, so consider that you may need to explain both the *content* and the *visualization type*. You might include a scatterplot in an academic journal, but that same visual type may not work in a report to a state policymaker.

An effective graph should tap into the brain's "preattentive visual processing." Because our eyes detect a limited set of visual characteristics, such as shape or contrast, we easily combine those characteristics and unconsciously perceive them as an image. In contrast to "attentive processing"—the conscious part of perception that allows us to perceive things serially—preattentive processing is done in parallel and is much faster. Preattentive processing allows the reader to perceive multiple basic visual elements simultaneously. Here is a simple example. Count the occurrences of the number 3 in the following set:

1269548523612356987458245

0124036985702069568312781

2439862012478136982173256

Now repeat the task with these two sets:

1269548523612356987458245   1269548523612356987458245

0124036985702069568312781   0124036985702069568312781

2439862012478136982173256   2439862012478136982173256

The 3s in these sets are much easier to find because they are encoded using a different preatttentive attribute—gray-shaded and boldface type on the left and color and boldface type on the right.

The same process applies when you are looking at graphs. Notice how adding a box around the *Forecast* area of this line chart (the pre-attentive attribute known as *enclosure*) helps draw your eye to the right side of the graph. The *position* and *color* attributes in this scatterplot help pull your attention to the circle off to the right.

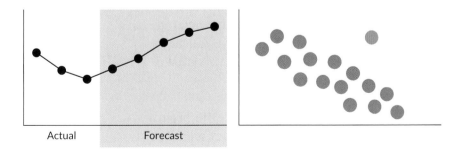

Actual   Forecast

Preattentive attributes like color, shape, enclosure, line width, and others are elements you should consider adding to (or removing from) your visualizations to help your reader more clearly see the important elements.

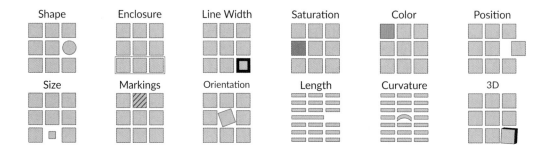

To create better, more effective graphs, I find it especially useful to follow three basic principles:

First, *show the data*. People are reading your graphs to better understand your argument or hypothesis. The data are the most important part of the graph and should be presented in the clearest way possible. That does not mean you should show *all* the data—indeed, many graphs show too much data, without making it clear to the reader which points or elements are most important.

Second, *reduce the clutter*. Chart clutter, or the use of unnecessary or distracting visual elements, makes your visualizations less effective. Clutter comes in the form of dark or heavy gridlines; unnecessary tick marks, labels, or text; unnecessary icons or pictures; ornamental shading and gradients; and unnecessary dimensions. Visualizations may contain textured or filled gradients, data markers, 3D perspectives, or other heavy elements that obscure the data and, therefore, the argument within the chart.

Third, *integrate graphics and text*. Use labels, active titles, and annotations on your charts to help the reader easily understand your argument. As a simple strategy, instead of using legends—which are often placed away from the content—directly label the lines, bars, or points. This makes it easier for your reader to understand what you are showing. Another simple strategy is to replace passive, nondescript titles with active, concise titles that help the reader quickly and easily obtain the purpose of the visualization.

These three principles embody the idea that, in most cases, you should help your reader quickly and easily acquire the information you wish to convey. By stripping out unnecessary clutter, emphasizing the data, and using certain preattentive attributes, your graphs can more clearly and effectively communicate information. Be purposeful about what you include in your visualizations so they best serve your reader and your message.

Keep in mind that graphs in research reports or articles, and even those in verbal presentations (see next chapter), are meant for *the audience*, not the author. The quick line graph you create for yourself while exploring the data—with default gridlines, tick marks, and colors—may not be the one that attracts and enlightens everyone else.

Applying the Principles: An Example

We can take these basic principles and apply them to any graph. Take the following line graph of median house prices in four U.S. cities over eight years. I've mimicked the default (and sometimes awkward) styling and labeling decisions people and software sometimes make. Notice how the clutter—year labels on the line for Boulder, boxed-out legend on the bottom right, and rotated axis labels—makes the graph less clear than it could be.

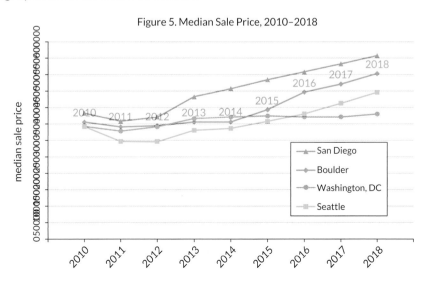

Figure 5. Median Sale Price, 2010–2018

To start, we can reduce the number of digits on the y-axis labels, rotate them horizontally, and reduce the number of labels and gridlines.

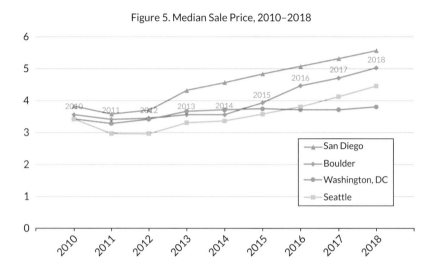

We can also adjust the horizontal axis by deleting the extra space before 2010 and after 2018 and rotating the axis labels. (I also deleted the vertical axis line, which is primarily a style choice; at the very least, I want to lighten it so it's not a visual anchor as in the original.)

Now let's remove the legend and the labels on the line for Boulder. Instead, we can directly label the lines for each city and remove the data markers. We can also change the colors so that they don't look like every other graph made with Microsoft Excel's default color palette.

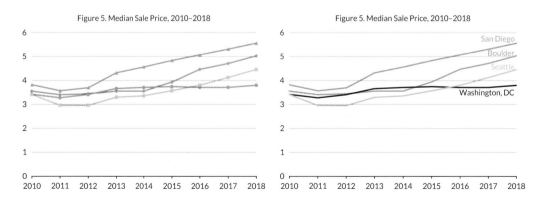

Finally, let's make the title active and tell the reader exactly what they are supposed to learn from the graph. We can also label the vertical axis label in the subtitle, which is now aligned horizontally and easier to read. We could also take a different look at the data and show the percent change as in the graph on the right—notice here how the last point is marked with the label for each city.

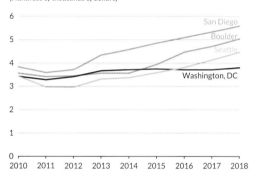

Figure 5. Median housing sale prices have slowed in Washington, DC
(Hundreds of thousands of dollars)

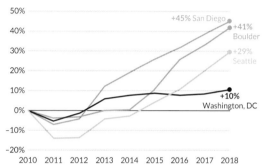

Figure 5. Median housing sale prices growth has slowed in Washington, DC
(Precent change since 2010)

Form and Function

One of the most important things you can do when visualizing your data is to consider the needs of your audience. Some audiences want the details of your analysis, regression results with standard errors and *t*-statistics; others want short summaries. Some audiences want to hear stories, while others want to access and analyze your data themselves. Consider who is most important, and target your visuals to meet their needs.

One way to think about the needs of your audience and how your visuals will help you reach them is to examine the different forms and functions of your data visualizations. Consider, for example, the vertical axis in the following image, which illustrates the connection between the two general *forms* of visualization. Static visualizations provide all the information at once and are not active or moving— charts that appear on paper, for example. Interactive visualizations allow users to select the information they want to see. These might be the visualizations you explore and click around on your computer or mobile phone. Animated visualizations, which move but do not necessarily permit manipulation of data points to create alternative results—such as movies and online slideshows where the user can control the pace of the story—can be thought of as falling between a static and an interactive visualization.

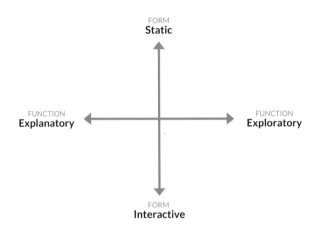

Now consider the horizontal *function* axis. Explanatory visualizations bring the main results to the forefront—they "surface key findings"— and help reveal the argument, hypothesis, or story. Exploratory visualizations help users interact with a dataset or subject matter to uncover findings themselves. Such visualizations do not generally propose a single narrative or draw out specific insights.

Researchers often live in a world of static explanatory graphs; their visualizations tend to reinforce single points of a narrative made in the accompanying text. Think of your standard line, bar, or pie chart. Infographics—a longer visual form that tends to combine text, graphics, pictures, and icons—also typically lie in this quadrant.

A static exploratory figure encourages readers to discover their own stories. Take this *Nobels, no degrees* infographic by Accurat Studios that I show in full and zoomed in below. The authors don't tell you a specific story or message; they expect you to explore the data through the visual.

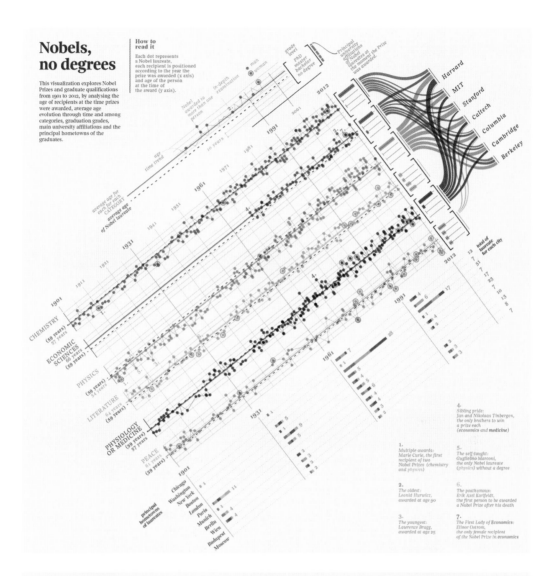

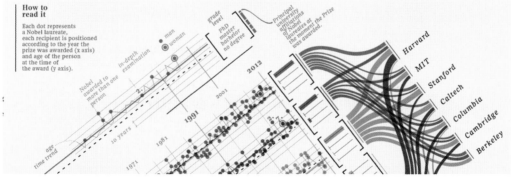

Source: Reproduced by permission of Accurat Studios, https://giorgialupi.wordpress
.com/2013/11/27/gold-medal-at-the-information-is-beautiful-design-award/.

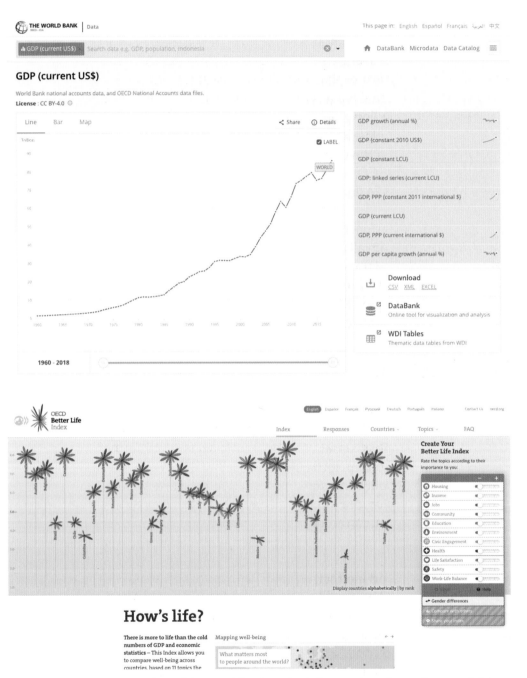

Source: Top: The World Bank (http://data.worldbank.org/topic/economic-policy-and-external-debt
.Bottom: The Organisation for Economic Co-Operation and Development (http://www.oecdbetterlife
-index.org).

Interactive visualizations are popular because they open up the possibility of new and independent conclusions. They also enable the user to take those discoveries and produce something more explanatory. Perhaps the easiest explanatory interactive graph type to consider is a static graph that has an interactive hover or rollover layered on top like the simple line graph from the World Bank on the top of the previous page. Exploratory interactive visualizations, such as the Better Life Index from the Organisation for Economic Co-operation and Development (OECD) at bottom, graphically present a complete dataset and ask users to find interesting stories.

Each axis in the form-function graphic is a *spectrum*. Visualizations can have elements from all four quadrants and enable the reader (or user) to explore the data, while also pointing toward the author's goal, hypothesis, and conclusions. The only "right" visualization type is the one that best meets the needs of your audience and helps you communicate information clearly and effectively to them.

Choosing a Graph

Poor graphs communicate ineffectively—or, even worse, provide a distorted impression of the data. Some decisions are subjective, of course: line thickness, series order, or axis label style, for example. The choice of a color palette, like the choice of a font, also can be subjective, but following some basic guidelines can improve communication. Other decisions, such as omitting unnecessary clutter and decoration, can result in objectively better ways to convey meaning.

One way to get around ineffective visual data communication is to use more types of graphs. You likely know how to read, and probably create, standard graphs like line charts, bar charts, and pie charts. But there are lots of other graphs out there for you to use. In some cases, these graphs will do a better job communicating your data, and in other cases they will help you create a different, more engaging graph type, which itself could be a goal.

Allow me to illustrate with an example. The data in these six graphs are all the same, but what you perceive and compare differs in each. In the pair of pie charts (option A), you might focus on the part-to-whole relationship—how much space each slice takes up in the pie. In the paired column chart (option B), you likely make comparisons *within* each group—the big downward shift in the Disagree category and the upward shift in the Strongly Agree category. Comparing *across* groups, however, is slightly harder.

One alternative is a diverging bar chart, in which the Disagree and Agree categories are aligned along a common vertical baseline and expanded in both directions (option C). In this view, you likely focus on the comparison of the *entire* Agree and Disagree categories rather than the individual components. Another alternative is a slope chart, which shows the difference between January 2016 and January 2017 by pairing the points on two vertical axes (option D). This view focuses less on the part-to-whole relationship (as in the pie charts) and more on the *change* over time.

Finally, there is a stacked bar chart and a waffle chart (options E and F). The stacked bar chart helps readers see the part-to-whole relationship, but it can be a little more difficult to compare the exact differences between each segment because they are not each aligned on the same axes. The waffle charts might be a bit more engaging, but it's harder to compare the specific categories between the two years.

Each graph has its own advantages and disadvantages, and there are best practices associated with each (e.g., the vertical axis in the column chart should start at zero). Which graph you like best should be determined by what relationship you are seeking to highlight for your reader. Enabling your reader to make exact comparisons between the values may, for example, lead you to the column chart. If you want to make something a bit more engaging and help your reader make general comparisons, the waffle chart may be your best bet.

A common question people learning data visualization ask is, "What is the right graph for my data?" Unfortunately, there is no definitive answer to this question because there is no one-to-one mapping between graph types and data types—a bar chart, for example, can be used to show changes over time or to show comparisons between different categories. A better question is, "What is the right graph for my data given *my stated purpose and audience*?" Once you start honing in on these more specific questions, you will be better able to choose the graph type that best fits your data and your goals.

How likely are you to buy a house this year?

Active Charts

There are three primary ways you can make your graphs more active to help your audience reach conclusions, see patterns, or make discoveries.

1. *Use Active Titles.* Your chart titles can give your readers the bottom-line point or argument. Don't be shy about adding subtitles that provide additional context or descriptive elements.

Notice how the Pew Research Center used a simple active title in this line chart. In an academic journal, this chart would be titled something like, "Figure 4. Labor force participation rates, Men and Women, 1950–2016." That's certainly true, but it doesn't help readers better understand what they're supposed to get out of this graph. The active title tells readers what the author wants them to learn.

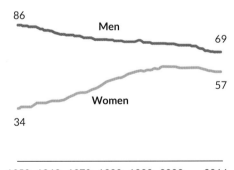

Labor force participation rate has risen for women, fallen for men

Labor force participation rate (%), among those ages 16 and older

86

Men

69

57

Women

34

1950 1960 1970 1980 1990 2000   2016

Note: Labor force participation rate is the share of the men and women working or looking for work.
Source: Bureau of Labor Statistics historical data.
"Wide Partisan Gaps in U.S. Over How Far the Country Has Come on Gender Equality"

PEW RESEARCH CENTER

Source: Pew Research Center, http://www.pewsocialtrends.org/2017/10/18/wide-partisan-gaps-in-u-s-over-how-far-the-country-has-come-on-gender-equality/.

2. Add Annotation. The implicit intention of many graph creators is, "Here you go, you figure it out." Instead, creators should help readers better understand the content or data. By adding annotation, you help your reader better understand the point of the visual and, if necessary, how to read the graph. Remember, if you've carefully considered your audience, you may recognize that some people will quickly and easily grasp how to read your chart and others may not.

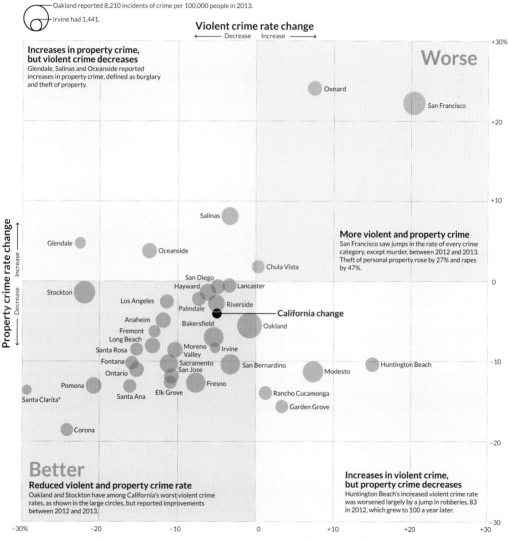

Source: Reproduced by permission of the *Los Angeles Times*, http://graphics.latimes.com/california-crime-2013/.

As an example, the bubble chart on the previous page was published by the *Los Angeles Times* in 2013. In it, the authors show the relationship between the change in violent crime rates (along the horizontal axis) and the change in property crime rates (along the vertical axis) for about 35 cities in California.

The average *Los Angeles Times* reader may not be familiar with this chart type, so the authors added some important annotations. The top-right quadrant is shaded red with a big red "Worse" and the bottom-left quadrant is shaded blue with a big blue "Better." Thus, even someone who has never seen a bubble chart before knows that the cities in the top-right are doing worse and those in the bottom-left are doing better. Each quadrant also contains a short, bold-faced headline with additional text that explains the content of the graphic. The annotation in this graph tells the reader both how to *read* the graph and how to *get content* from the graph.

3. *Start with Gray*. A practical approach I like to use in my work is to start all my graphs completely in gray. This forces me, the content creator, to be strategic and purposeful in what I want the reader to get out of the graph.

In a research project I conducted a couple of years ago, I was interested in exploring the high proportion of people in the six New England states who receive benefits through the U.S. Social Security Disability Insurance program because of a mental disorder diagnosis, such as developmental disorders, mood disorders, or schizophrenia. I didn't just want to show the patterns for those six states on their own, because they wouldn't capture the relatively higher rate of receipt for people in these states compared with others around the country.

I started with this line chart that shows the "recipiency rate" (the percentage of 18- to 65-year-olds in each state that receives benefits) for every state in the country. Produced using the basic default settings in Microsoft Excel, you can make out the general pattern of an increase over time. And if you were to look very carefully, you might be able to distinguish one state from another (assuming, of course, I gave you the big legend with 50 states). But seeing that Massachusetts, Rhode Island, and the other New England states are higher than the rest of the country is just not clear.

Social Security Disability Insurance recipiency rate for mental disorders rose swiftly in New England states between 2001 and 2015
(percent)

Source: Author's calculations based on data from the Social Security Administration, 2002–2016.

When I make all the lines gray, however, as shown on the next page, you could never figure out which line applies to which state (even if I gave you the legend!). You can't identify any individual series or see the overall point I'm trying to convey (captured in the active title).

But with the lines all gray, I can start adding color, shapes, markings, or other attributes to show the most important series. In this case, because I wanted to highlight the six New England states, I colored and labeled just those lines (plus the line for the nation as a whole).

The *start with gray* approach forces you to be thoughtful about what you want your graphs to ultimately achieve. You can either physically change the elements to gray or (at least) imagine what would happen when the various elements were all the same color. Then you can implement the visual elements to help direct your reader's attention where you want it.

Social Security Disability Insurance recipiency rate for mental disorders rose swiftly in New England states between 2001 and 2015
(percent)

Source: Author's calculations based on data from the Social Security Administration, 2002–2016.

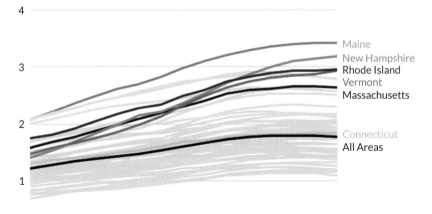

Social Security Disability Insurance recipiency rate for mental disorders rose swiftly in New England states between 2001 and 2015
(percent)

Source: Author's calculations based on data from the Social Security Administration, 2002–2016.

Alternative Chart Types

Most people who work with data are familiar with the basic graph types like lines, bars, and pies. Other chart types are used less frequently, likely because they are not readily available in many standard software programs like Microsoft Excel. These other nonstandard chart types can be useful not because they are inherently *better* than the standard types but because sometimes seeing data in different ways can engage readers or help them see patterns they may not notice in other chart types. Though there are many, many graphs to choose from, here are four alternatives that I find especially useful (the box at the end of this chapter lists some additional resources).

Dot Plot. In a dot plot, points are placed along an axis designating two or more values. On one axis sit the categories, which can be ranked or sorted, but the heights do not typically correspond to a data value. On the other axis sit the data values. The points are typically connected by a thin line or arrow. The dot plot is a good alternative to pairs of columns or bars because it enables the reader to see both the level and the change.

The graphs on the next page show mathematics test scores from the National Assessment of Educational Progress for 20 states in 2017. There are two sets of scores, an unadjusted number and a number adjusted for demographic differences such as race, receipt of special education services, and status as English language learner. The bar chart on top looks heavy and cluttered, which makes it difficult to discern the overall ranking across states and the differences within states. It's easier to accomplish both tasks with the dot plot on the bottom which has more white space and less clutter. This dot plot is sorted by the *adjusted* value, but it could also be sorted by the *unadjusted* value, the gap between the two, or some other ordering. (You'll also notice that the horizontal axis of the bar chart starts at zero because the preattentive attribute we use to perceive the values is the length of the bars. In the dot plot, the horizontal axis starts at the lowest value because we use the relative position of the dots to perceive those values.)

Unadjusted v. adjusted scores   ▪ Unadjusted ▪ Adjusted

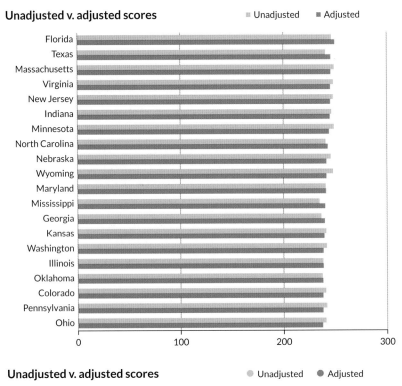

Unadjusted v. adjusted scores   ● Unadjusted ● Adjusted

2017 4th grade math with controls for age, race or ethnicity, special education status, free and reduced-price lunch eligibility (imputed), and English language learner status

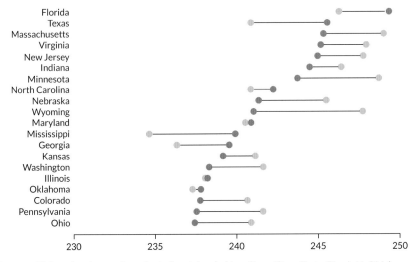

Source: Urban Institute, *America's Gradebook: How Does Your State Stack Up?* Urban Institute, 2018, http://apps.urban.org/features/naep/.

Heatmap. A heatmap uses ranges of colors or shades to represent differences in values. Darker shades correspond to higher values and lighter shades to lower values. Heatmaps are especially useful when you have a lot of data or high-frequency data. They are often most useful when you are trying to visualize *general* patterns or trends and are not as worried about enabling the reader to ascertain specific values. In the following visualization, vehicle fatalities are displayed using this heatmap format laid out like a calendar. You can see the greater number of fatalities on the right edge of each month (i.e., the weekends) in the darker shades of blue. The line graph on the right shows the same data with Saturdays highlighted in dark blue circles. Same data, different visual approach, but here, the heatmap is a *better* choice. Yes, it's a nonstandard graph type, but it likely engages you in ways the line chart doesn't and, more important, it's easier to see the patterns.

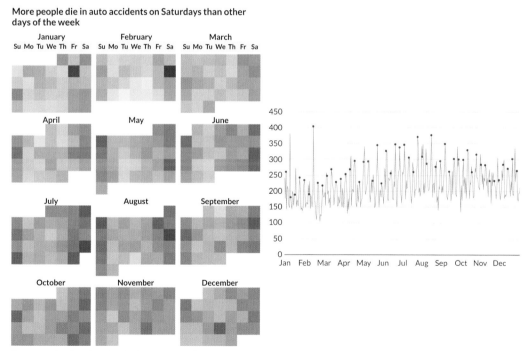

More people die in auto accidents on Saturdays than other days of the week

Source: Author's calculations using data from the National Highway Traffic Safety Administration. Calendar layout inspired by Nathan Yau at FlowingData.com.

Tile Grid Map. A tile grid map assigns an equally sized shape (such as squares or hexagons) to each geographic unit, regardless of its actual size. One disadvantage of the typical "choropleth" map—in which color is applied to the geographic units to denote the data values—is that the importance of the data and the geographic space may not correspond. In the United States, for example, Wyoming has three electoral votes and Connecticut has seven, but in square miles, the former is more than 17 times larger than the latter. The tile grid map makes all geographic units the same size, which helps overcome this particular distortion. On the flip side, however, choropleth maps are familiar to people and make it easy to identify where we live and work, a task harder to accomplish with the tile grid map. In this simple example of state unemployment rates in the United States, all states show up as equal-sized squares with the shades of blue denoting the values.

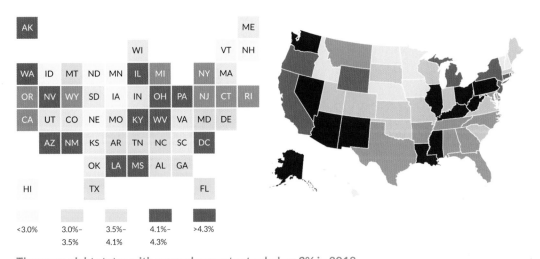

There are eight states with unemployment rates below 3% in 2018

Source: Author's calculations based on data from the Bureau of Labor Statistics.

Waffle Chart. A waffle chart is a set of aligned squares, typically divided into a 10×10 grid to visualize percentages. Typically, a waffle chart uses squares, but it could also use circles, triangles, or other icons. These four waffle charts show the labor force participation rates for black and white men and women in March 2018. Each square represents a single percentage point; the blue and yellow areas denote the total value (also added in the title for each grid) and the gray squares fill the remaining space.

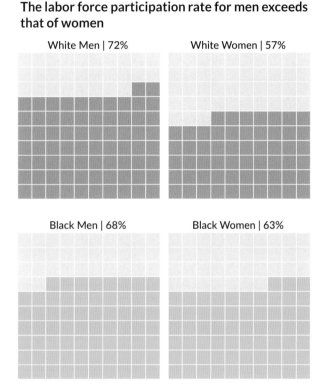

Source: Author's calculations using data from the Bureau of Labor Statistics.

Data Visualization Tools

You may have noticed that I haven't mentioned how I made the graphs in this chapter or which tools are best to do so. There is a wide range of software tools you can use to create data visualizations, from drag-and-drop tools like Microsoft Excel and Tableau to programming languages like JavaScript, Python, and R. No single tool is necessarily better than another; it depends on your (and your organization's) workflow and skill-set, and what you need to create. Simple, static graphs might be best created in a drag-and-drop tool like Excel whereas more complex, interactive visualizations will likely need to be built in JavaScript or one of the many tools based in JavaScript.

This list is not a comprehensive accounting of all the tools you can use to create visualizations. As of the time of this writing, these tools appear to be the most popular and commonly used.

Drag-and-Drop. These tools allow the user to create charts by using relatively simple interfaces with which you can insert and style charts, create tables, or even prepare interactive visualizations. Drag-and-drop tools are great because you can quickly and easily create visualizations, often of very high quality. But you can only go so far with such tools because you are restricted to the menus and capabilities of the tool, even if you can "hack" into the background charting engine. Examples include Microsoft Excel and PowerBI, Tableau, and the online platform Infogram.

Programming Languages. Programming languages allow you almost infinite flexibility but have a much steeper learning curve than drag-and-drop tools. Traditional statistical software programming languages such as Stata and SAS have basic charting engines. Other languages like Python and R have some elements of statistical analysis but also have sophisticated (and growing) data visualization capabilities. Perhaps the most common programming language to create interactive visualizations is the D3 library as part of the JavaScript programming language.

Mix of Drag-and-Drop and Programming Languages. Some tools mix the drag-and-drop interface with programming languages. Excel and Tableau, for example, have behind-the-scenes programming languages you can use to extend the capabilities of the tool (Visual Basic for Applications in Excel and Calculated Fields in Tableau). Other tools are typically built on top of JavaScript, which can enable you to create interactive visualizations with limited or no coding. DataWrapper, Flourish, HighCharts, Lyra, Plotly, and RAW are examples of tools that combine drag-and-drop features with some programming.

Mapping Tools. Visualizing geographic data is often challenging because good mapping tools are expensive, hard to use, or overly simplified. Again, programming languages such as R and D3 will give you the most flexibility, whereas tools specifically built for mapping like ESRI and Mapbox have more capabilities. Spreadsheet programs like Excel and PowerBI, Tableau, and Google Sheets can be used to create basic maps.

Color Tools. Choosing colors for a visualization or design project can be a daunting task, especially if you don't have a design background. There is a wide array of online (and free) color choosing tools that you can use to help develop a single color or full-color palette. Adobe's Color tool is a popular and easy-to-use tool that allows you to create an entire palette from the standard color wheel. Other tools such as Color Brewer, Colour Lovers, Colrd, and Paletton work in similar ways.

Wrapping Up

For researchers, scholars, and practitioners who want their readers to comprehend their work quickly and accurately, presentation matters. Effective data visualizations show the data to highlight important findings, reduce clutter to keep the focus on the important points, and integrate text with the graphs to communicate information efficiently. With the increased flexibility of even fairly basic software programs, it now costs less in time and energy for scholars and analysts to invest some time learning and thinking about graphical presentation.

To create great, effective visualizations, carefully consider the needs of your audience—the numbers, facts, or stories that will help them understand your ideas and your arguments. Consider the interfaces—static versus interactive—they will use. And pair the depth and clarity of your data, models, and writing with visualizations that are just as clear and compelling.

Key Takeaways

- Always consider your audience. Visualizations for an academic journal article will be very different than those you show to a policymaker or a reporter.
- Drive your reader's attention where you want it by carefully and purposefully using colors, lines, markings, and other visual elements.
- Make your charts active through good, concise titles and useful annotations.
- Don't get bogged down by the same old graphs time and time again; lots of different graph types out there might help reveal interesting patterns or insights in your data.

Data Visualization Books

If you want to learn more about data visualization, there are some great books that dive deeper into the topics discussed in this chapter.

Alberto Cairo. Author of two books specifically about data visualization, *The Functional Art* and *The Truthful Art*, and another (*How Charts Lie*) about how members of the public can become more informed readers of graphs. Cairo is a journalism professor, so his books focus primarily on creating data visualizations for telling stories to a wide audience. The books provide overviews of data, data visualization, introductory statistics, and how to create visualizations.

Jorge Camões. His book *Data at Work* covers a wide range of data visualization principles and strategies, ranging from rules of visual perception to design considerations to data preparation and visualization.

Stephen Few. Author of several books on data visualization, his *Show Me the Numbers* and *Now You See It: Simple Visualization Techniques for Quantitative Analysis* are comprehensive synopses of how to present data effectively and strategically.

Andy Kirk. Author of two books on data visualization, his latest, *Data Visualisation: A Handbook for Data Driven Design* outlines a system to conceptualize and develop data visualizations, and a process to help readers make design choices that result in clear and effective visualizations.

Cole Nussbaumer Knaflic. Knaflic's book *Storytelling with Data*, and blog of the same name, provides an introductory treatment of data visualization and how to pair text with graphs to tell effective, compelling stories.

Claus Wilke. Wilke's *Fundamentals of Data Visualization* dives deeper into some of the less standard graph types and shows some best practices of basic data visualizations.

Dona Wong. Wong's *Guide to Information Graphics* dedicates individual pages to specific graph types, how and why to choose the best chart to fit the data, the most effective way to communicate data, and what to include and not include in different graphs.

Case Study: *Readers devour an easily digestible data visualization*

When researchers consider creating a data visualization, they can sometimes be intimidated by the thought of an elaborate feature with lots of bells, whistles, and interactivity. But a data visualization doesn't need to be complicated to be effective. In fact, one of the Urban Institute's most-viewed features has some of the simplest graphics.

When Urban researchers noticed that wealth inequality was becoming a hot topic in the news, they wanted to seize the chance to attract attention to their work. They decided to produce a visual research product to illustrate why wealth inequality hadn't improved over the past 50 years.

The resulting feature—*Nine Charts about Wealth Inequality in America*—illustrated Urban research findings through an accessible narrative and nine simple charts. Each chart made a single point, which was emphasized in short, descriptive headings so the findings were easy to digest. One graph had light animation, but most had limited interactivity, and only when it was necessary to make a point. Overall, the graphs were free of clutter and easy to understand, which, coupled with the timeliness of the subject matter, helped explain why the feature was so popular.

Prioritizing simplicity paid off. The feature has received hundreds of thousands of views and has been cited by numerous media outlets. In 2017, the researchers received funding to update the charts so they can continue to help ground the conversation about wealth inequality in the latest data and evidence.

The success of the *Nine Charts about Wealth Inequality* feature shows that a data visualization project doesn't need to be complicated to tell a story about your research. There are times when a story is best told through animation or interactivity, but even static charts can be powerful tools. With a little creativity, you can use data visualizations without breaking the bank. It may just be the most widely viewed project you've ever created.

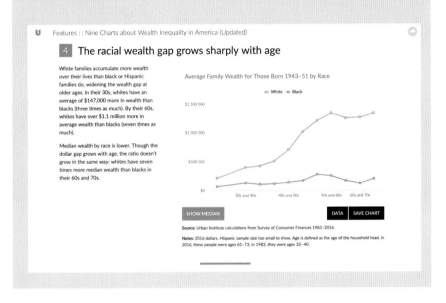

chapter four

Better Presentations: More Effective Speaking

Jonathan Schwabish

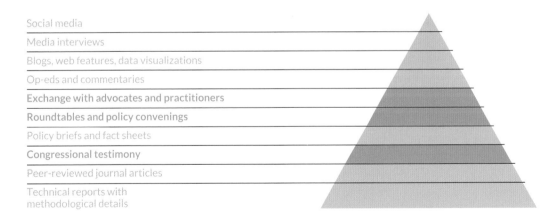

Many researchers follow a familiar pattern when they are asked to present their work to an audience: First, they open PowerPoint. Second, they start adding text—it might be new text, but it's more likely pasted from the written report—into bullet points on the slide. Third, they copy and paste graphs or tables—again, often directly from the report. Finally, they create a concluding slide that says "Questions?" or "Thank You!," save the file, and consider themselves ready to present.

There is a better way to present your research. It doesn't matter if it's a lunchtime meeting with your colleagues, a 15-minute conference presentation, or a keynote address in front of hundreds of people. It starts with recognizing that a presentation is not about the *speaker*, but the *audience*. Once you realize that the primary goal of your presentation is to convince the audience of your ideas, hypotheses, and conclusions, you can think about how to more effectively get them to believe you.

A presentation is a fundamentally different form of communication than a written report. When your reader sits down with your report, she can read at her own pace, take notes, highlight, and explore the tables, graphs, or formulas in detail. As a member of an audience, however, she is bound by *your* pace and how you present the information.

The shift toward an audience-centric presentation has three driving principles:

First, visualize your content. The way our eyes and brains work together allows us to better grasp and retain information through pictures rather than just through words (this is known as the "picture superiority effect"). Countless research has tested how people recall words, categories, and text, and how quickly and accurately they do so. Recall the "preattentive processing" concept from Chapter 3, in which employing attributes such as color, position, and line width help draw attention to a particular region of an image. The same is true in a presentation; as a presenter, you can harness the power of pictures to create well-designed slides and better data visualizations to help your audience remember and understand more of what you say.

Second, unify the elements of your presentation. This means consistency in your use of colors and fonts, in the layout and format of your slides, and in integrating what you say with what you show on the screen. Slide design is not about "dumbing down" your presentation or sacrificing content in the name of making things "pop"; it's about using color, images, and layout to help structure information in a way that helps the audience better understand your work. If you toss in a random slide with different colors, different fonts, and a different tone or feel, it can disrupt the flow of the presentation, which disrupts the flow of information and your audience's ability to absorb your content. Your presentation slides are there to support you, not supplant you.

Finally, focus your audience's attention on your argument. This principle is perhaps the most important. Instead of putting up as much information as possible on every slide—which many presenters do because it's easy and it reminds them to cover each point—keep your slides simple and free of clutter so you can direct your audience's attention where you want it at all times. You can increase the amount of information your audience recognizes and recalls by helping them focus on a specific point, be it text, data, image, or spoken information.

These three principles—visualize, unify, and focus—all aim to facilitate the audience's quick and easy acquisition of information. By designing high-quality slides and pairing your spoken word with those visuals, you help your audience can focus on what's really important—namely, your content and your message—rather than make them waste their energy and attention trying to decipher what's on the screen and how it relates to what you are trying to say.

Planning Your Presentation

Every presentation should start with careful, strategic planning. What do you hope to accomplish with your talk? Do you want people to fund your research? Do you want them to use your ideas in their work? Do you want them to give you access to more data? Are you trying to further the field? Before you can deliver an effective presentation, you need to know *why* you are giving the talk and *what* you want people to do with the information.

Researchers often balk at the idea of "selling" themselves or their work: We're not designers, we're not salespeople: we're researchers!

But, remember, when you present your research to an audience, you are in effect *selling* your work—that your ideas and hypotheses are sound, that your data are used correctly, that your methods are reasonable. In that vein, consider your presentation as your opportunity to get your audience to "buy" into your ideas.

To begin, don't simply turn on your computer, boot up PowerPoint or your favorite presentation software tool, and start typing. Instead, start by considering what you want to convey to your audience and how you want to do so. In other words, start building your presentation by planning and outlining what it is you want your presentation to accomplish and what it is you want to present. If you have, say, 15 minutes at a conference or 5 minutes in front of a funder to present the results from your 50-page report, you should immediately recognize that everything is not going to fit. What are the most important points? What content will help convince your audience of your ideas?

Presentation Worksheet

The following 10-question worksheet can help you plan your presentation before you start building it. The worksheet guides you through the various sections and important elements of your presentation. You can also download a copy of the worksheet for your own use from the book's website (https://www.urban.org/ElevatetheDebateBook).

> 1. What type of presentation are you giving?
>
>   ❑ Small meeting   ❑ Keynote address
>   ❑ Department or conference seminar   ❑ Workshop
>   ❑ Classroom lecture   ❑ Other
>   ❑ Sales pitch/funding request

Tailor the style, look, and message of your presentation to the event and venue. You may focus on specific details and methodology at your department's lunchtime seminar with 20 people, but you are probably better off focusing on the broad points and key messages in a keynote address in front of a few hundred people.

2. Who is your audience?

❏ Co-workers or colleagues   ❏ Students
❏ Managers   ❏ Mixed
❏ Scientists/technical professionals   ❏ Other
❏ Salespeople and marketers

Like the first, this question encourages you to think carefully about how your audience will benefit from your presentation. You will likely focus on different things when you present to your colleagues than when you present to a decisionmaker or funder, or even students. The language you use will also differ: technical jargon and abbreviations may work for one group but not another.

3. What is the headline message of your presentation?

I give myself space for a single sentence here—boil the idea down to its essential core. In his book *The Presentation Secrets of Steve Jobs*, author Carmine Gallo refers to these as "Twitter-like" headlines: specific, memorable, concise headlines that your audience can easily remember and share. It's not about "dumbing things down," it's about finding the most important part of your work.

4. What do you want your audience to do with your conclusions?

Consider both your audience and your main goal in giving your presentation. What do you want your audience to do with your work and your results? Do you want them to adopt your results and put them into practice? Use your data? Fund more of your work? You may not need to state your goal explicitly in your talk, but specifically considering your goals can help you construct a more effective and targeted presentation.

5. Craft your opening statement.

You don't have long to grab and keep your audience's attention. Instead of starting your presentation with some pleasantries like, "Thanks for having me," or "I'm happy to be here," begin with your takeaway message and the importance of that message. Immediately engage your audience by talking about why your work is important and why they should care.

6. Craft your closing statement.

The beginning and ending of your presentation are when you have your audience's maximum attention, so treat those moments carefully. Your closing statement is your opportunity to sum up the most important points from your presentation and highlight the message you want everyone to take away.

7. Outline the sections of your presentation.
1.
2.
3.
4.
5.

I leave space for five sections here. You may need fewer, but avoid having many more because too many sections can make it hard for your audience to follow your presentation. You can think of these sections as "chapter titles," and, like chapter titles, each should be oriented around a distinct idea and point.

8. What stories can you tell?

Another way to relate to and engage your audience is to link your work to relevant stories. By our very nature, we are drawn to the narrative structure of stories, and they can increase your audience's attention by making it easier for them to relate to you and remember your content.

9. Images (sketch or describe before searching)
   ❑ Graphs and charts
   ❑ Pictures, illustrations, and icons
   ❑ Videos

You probably have data-driven graphs and charts from your written report or other places, but you need to modify them for a presentation. People interact with graphs in a written report in very different ways than they do in a presentation. When it comes to pictures, illustrations, icons, and videos, a specific idea of what you're looking for will help you find relevant, useful images. Don't let the Internet tell you what image works best for "educating children"; instead, consider what images you think would work best for your content and then go find them. By sketching and describing your own ideas for the images you want to use, you, not your Internet search engine, will be control of your visuals. I have included some of my favorite image websites in the *Design Resources Box* at the end of this chapter.

10. Anticipated Q&A
    1. Q:

       A:

    2. Q:

       A:

Think about possible questions you may receive and craft your answers. The worksheet includes space for you to list two questions, but you should obviously be prepared to answer more. You may already be aware of the shortcomings of your work or the things you needed to leave out in your 15-minute talk. Perhaps you're presenting to a specific audience—funders, the media, or decisionmakers—and can anticipate additional concerns these stakeholders may have.

Completing the worksheet and expanding sections where necessary will give you the road map for your presentation. You can then start filling in the gaps and figuring out how to build the narrative of your work over your presentation.

Designing Your Slides

Now that you have outlined and prepared what you want to put in your slides, it's time to start designing them. The idea is not to become a designer yourself, but to learn some basic aspects of good slide design such as color, font, and layout, and integrate them in your presentations. My goal is to show you *why* you should create more effective slides and *how* to do so in easier and faster ways. For more resources on how to employ good design techniques in your slides, see the *Presentation Books* box at the end of this chapter.

There are five main classes of slides: text, data visualization, tables, images, and a group I call scaffolding slides. There are ways to improve the standard versions of each of these slide types.

The Text Slide: Use Less Text

The way many people convert their report or journal article to a presentation is to copy and paste from the written document: topic sentences become bullet points and graphs get copied onto slides. Quick and easy, and you're all set! Including too much text on your slides, however, ignores the very audience-centric approach good presenters use.

Each of your slides should have a single goal. This compels your audience to focus on your most important points and not become distracted by different numbers, topics, or text. When you show your audience a slide packed with dense text and bullet points, they are inclined to read it and stop paying attention to you.

One easy way you can improve your text slides is to break them up into multiple slides; this can be a very powerful way to encourage your audience to focus on your most important points. I call this the *layering* approach—the general philosophy is to show each point (goal) on its own. Together, you eventually come back to the original slide, but you have focused your audience's attention so they can read quickly and turn their attention back to you. This single slide, for example, can be broken up into four slides, graying out each bullet point when you are done discussing it (as shown on the next page).

Policy challenges

- *Rebalancing the policy mix*
  - Weak global growth and fiscal consolidation are weighing on prospects
  - Monetary policy is overburdened
  - Systemic financial risks remain
- *Strengthening productivity growth*
  - Poor state of infrastructure is holding back productivity
  - Business dynamism and entrepreneurship have weakened
  - Incumbents have acquired more market power
- *Reducing inequality*
  - Closing the wage gap between men and women
  - Providing opportunities for people of all races and ethnicities
- *Making growth more inclusive and sustainable*
  - Children from poor families lack the opportunity to do better than their parents
  - Women's opportunities will improve further, but the pace could be faster
  - Reduce social and racial inequalities
  - Helping displaced workers is gaining importance
  - Meeting COP21 carbon emission goals

Source: Original slide based on slides from the OECD, http://www.oecd.org/eco/surveys/economic-survey-united-states.htm.

Perhaps an even better approach is to make your text slides more visual. Try turning text-dense slides into graphs. Or remove passages of text and put them in your speaker notes (either using the speaker notes feature in your slide software or written out in front of you). By cutting down on the amount of text you show, you encourage your audience to pay attention to you rather than your slides.

An example of the layering approach.

Source: Original slide based on slides from the OECD, http://www.oecd.org/eco/surveys/economic-survey-united-states.htm.

To demonstrate, the way I might start remaking this slide from the OECD is to reduce the amount of text. I can keep the four major bullet points and remove the 13 sub-bullet points. If the presenter prepares and practices, we shouldn't need all that text.

With just four main bullet points, I can now redesign the slide. I make the title much larger and place the bullet-point text in a 2×2 matrix. I can add a bit of a design touch by making the title even bigger, changing the font (this one is called ChunkFive) and placing it on top of an orange banner.

Next, I use the *Visualize* principle and add some icons to the slide. I downloaded the icons from the Noun Project (https://thenoun project.com/) and placed each in circles drawn in PowerPoint. On the right, I add a subtle gray background gradient, which isn't totally necessary but could soften the slide if I were presenting in a small, dark room where a white background can seem blinding.

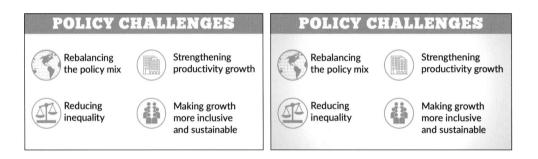

If I were in a large room or wanted a more sophisticated look, I might use a dark background and change the text color from black to white. I could also replace the plain black background with a photograph and add a dark tint so the text and icons are still visible.

Photo by Katie Moum on Unsplash.

The Data Visualization Slide: Make Good Graphs

Just as many presenters include too much text with bullet point after bullet point, so do many others show graphs and charts that are far too detailed or complex for a presentation. Remember, your audience is bound to *your* pace and content; if they have never seen the information before—or seen it presented in this way—they need time to absorb and understand how you are presenting it.

The Data Visualization chapter showed you some basic principles to make better, more effective visualizations. The three guiding principles in that chapter—Show the Data, Reduce Clutter, and Integrate Graphics and Text—still apply to presentations, but remember that a presentation is a fundamentally different form of communication than a written document. Therefore, dense, complex graphs that may work in your report or journal article may need to be changed, simplified, or edited when shown on the screen.

As with text, you can also *layer* your data visualizations. Take the simple line chart of median house prices from the previous chapter (on the left). In a presentation, data visualizations can be difficult for your audience to wade through—just like with text, the more time they need to spend deciphering what's going on in your slide, the less they can pay attention to you. Notice how in the slide version on the right, I have made all the text bigger and removed the "Figure 5" from the title—simple changes that show I am thinking about how this graph will be perceived when projected rather than read in a report.

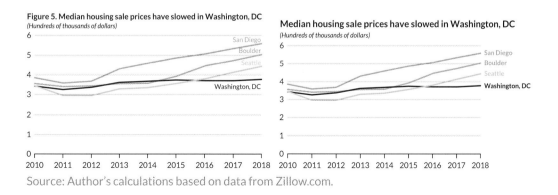

Figure 5. Median housing sale prices have slowed in Washington, DC
(Hundreds of thousands of dollars)

Median housing sale prices have slowed in Washington, DC
(Hundreds of thousands of dollars)

Source: Author's calculations based on data from Zillow.com.

There are a few ways to make data visualization slides even easier for your audience. You can layer each line (or bar or point) one at a time, focusing your audience's attention on each element as you add it to the final graph.

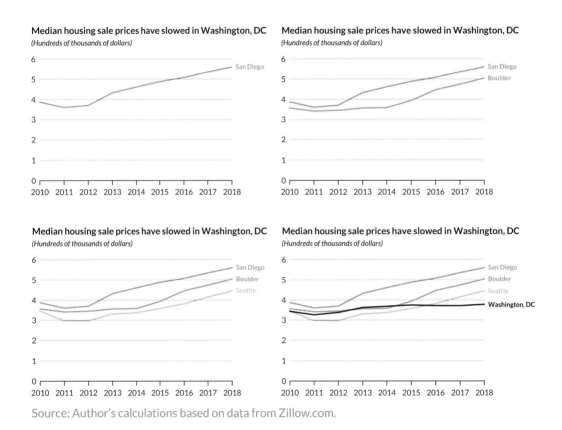

Source: Author's calculations based on data from Zillow.com.

Alternatively, you can use a single slide and highlight the most important data series and de-emphasize the others—using grays (recall the *Start with Gray* section from the previous chapter) is often a useful, easy strategy to fade various elements to the background.

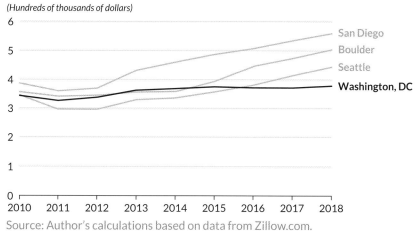

Median housing sale prices have slowed in Washington, DC
(Hundreds of thousands of dollars)

Source: Author's calculations based on data from Zillow.com.

In cases where you show a new graph type or a particularly complex graph, you might first just show the axes, describe how the graph is to be read, and then layer the data on the next slide or set of slides, as in this next example. Your audience of colleagues may be completely familiar with a bubble chart, but it might take an audience less familiar with the graph or content longer to understand what you are showing.

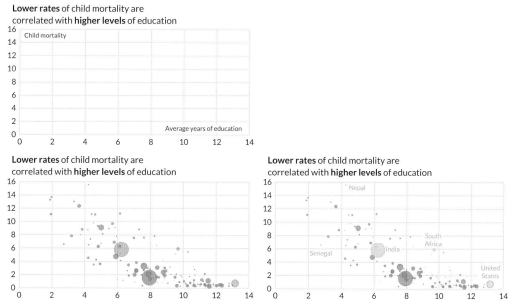

Source: Author's calculations using data from *Our World in Data,*
https://ourworldindata.org/recent-improvements-to-interactive-scatterplots.

The Table Slide: Simplify

Just as lots of presenters copy and paste text and graphs from the report into the slides, many do the same with tables. This technique might be even more problematic because many tables have *lots* of information—regression coefficients, standard errors, asterisks, notes, column and row headers and subheaders, and on and on. Again, your audience is going to try to decipher what's going on in Appendix Table 1—if they can see it. One of the worst things you can say in a presentation is, "I know you can't read this, but . . . "

The layering technique doesn't work here. The text is still too small, so showing one row or column at a time isn't going to help someone in the back of the room. A better approach is to altogether rethink the table. Consider which numbers are most important and *focus* your audience's attention. If you are sharing a set of regression results, for example, some estimates are likely not central to your argument—monthly dummy variables, say, may be important for the math but not necessarily for the relationship(s) you are trying to highlight. As with the headline for your entire presentation, figure out the headline message of your results, then decide how to best present those numbers. Leave the rest for questions or your report.

Alternatively, you could try to *visualize* your table results by converting them in to a graph or other visual. Depending on how much detail you want to cover, you could then apply the *layering* technique to the slide and show the four estimates for the first model, then the estimates for the second model, and so on.

Some researchers avoid using photographs, illustrations, or icons in their presentations because they think it takes away from the seriousness of their content. Images can serve an important function in presentations, however, because the audience will learn and remember more when your spoken word is combined with an image than left alone (this is known as the picture superiority effect and is

Table 6. Regression Results

	1	2	3	4
Gender	1.067	1.067	1.049	1.044
	(0.201)**	(0.250)**	(0.214)**	(0.281)**
Age	0.982	0.982	1.039	0.988
	(0.300)**	(0.320)**	(0.383)**	(0.312)**
Age^2	1.000	1.000	1.000	1.001
	(0.000)**	(0.000)**	(0.000)**	(0.000)**
Married	0.983	0.983	0.987	0.987
	(0.001)**	(0.001)**	(0.001)**	(0.001)**
Race	1.006	0.997	1.005	1.006
	(0.002)**	(0.002)+	(0.002)**	(0.002)**
Average Earnings	0.978	0.979	0.914	0.911
	(0.051)**	(0.083)**	(0.123)**	(0.181)**
GDP per capita	1.195	1.199	1.096	1.106
	(0.024)**	(0.024)**	(0.022)**	(0.022)**
Less than High School	1.613	1.609	1.477	1.493
	(0.023)**	(0.023)**	(0.021)**	(0.021)**
High School Graduate	1.325	1.327	1.176	1.166
	(0.037)**	(0.037)**	(0.032)**	(0.031)**
Some College	1.448	1.451	1.368	1.368
	(0.032)**	(0.032)**	(0.029)**	(0.029)**
Own a House	1.191	1.187	1.104	1.112
	(0.016)**	(0.016)**	(0.015)**	(0.015)**
Employed Full-Time	0.96	0.957	0.914	0.924
	(0.016)*	(0.016)**	(0.015)**	(0.015)**
Eastern Area	3.651	3,645	3.174	3.161
	(0.196)**	(0.196)**	(0.158)**	(0.156)**
Western Area	1.651	1.649	1.504	1.514
	(0.040)**	(0.040)**	(0.036)**	(0.036)**
Southern Area	1.229	1.225	1.216	1.225
	(0.031)**	(0.031)**	(0.030)**	(0.030)**
Year dummy variables[e]	No	No	Yes	Yes
Age dummy variables	No	No	No	Yes
No. of observations	37,678	37,678	36,640	36,080

Regression Results: Gender, Age, and Earnings are Positive and Statistically Significant

	1	2	3	4
Gender	1.067	1.067	1.049	1.044
	(0.201)**	(0.250)**	(0.214)**	(0.281)**
Age	0.982	0.982	1.039	0.988
	(0.300)**	(0.320)**	(0.383)**	(0.312)**
Average Earnings	0.978	0.979	0.914	0.911
	(0.051)**	(0.083)**	(0.123)**	(0.181)**
Number of Observations	37,678	37,678	36,640	36,080

supported by research on cognitive-load theory and different learning principles from researchers like Alan Paivio, John Sweller, and Richard Mayer).

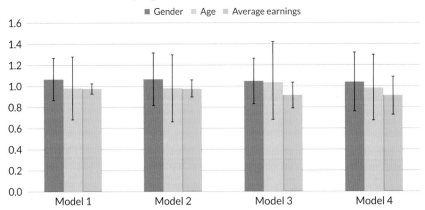

Regression Results: Gender, Age, and Earnings are Positive and Statistically Significant

The Image Slide: Use Good, Large Images

In general, take advantage of your entire slide space instead of using the default image size. Maximizing the image (or images) to fill the entire slide will make it easier for your audience to see them while reducing unnecessary blank space. The same strategy applies to multiple images: arrange and unify them with the text to fill the full space, instead of randomly placing them on the slide.

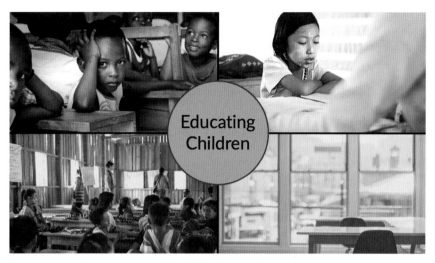

Photos (clockwise from top-left) by Bill Wegener, Peter Hershey, Matt Hoffman, NeONBRAND on Unsplash.

Lots of websites offer high-quality—often free—photographs, illustrations, and icons (see the *Design Resources* box at the end of this chapter). There is no need to use outdated clip art, bad stock images, or stretched or otherwise distorted pictures. Take time to consider which image will best help you convey your content, and find high-quality images to support that effort.

You can also use icons to make your slides more engaging and memorable. Icons can be a simple replacement for bullet points (recall the OECD slides previously) or visual anchors for your entire presentation. For example, you might use an icon of a house to introduce a topic and use it throughout your talk.

Scaffolding Slides: Build the Frame Around Your Content

There is one final set of slides to use in your presentation: Scaffolding slides help guide and focus your audience's attention as you transition from one section to another, and help you drive home important points. There are five different scaffolding slides you can use: the *title* and *agenda* slides to introduce your presentation, *header* slides to divide your presentation into sections, *breaker* slides that direct attention back to you, and *ending* slides for concluding your presentation.

Title Slide. Your title slide—which may be the one shown the longest as people filter into the room and settle in—can help set the tone of your talk. Use the opportunity to emphasize that you intend to deliver a substantive, engaging, and enjoyable presentation in which attendees will take away valuable content. Instead of simply putting the paper title and your name and contact information on a blank slide, can you include complementary images to help reinforce your content? Reduce the amount of unnecessary text on the slide— phone number, address, date—and kick off your presentation with something more memorable.

Photo by Marcelo Leal on Unsplash.

Agenda Slide. The more prepared your audience is for how you are going to deliver your message, the better they will follow along. Agenda slides can provide this road map, but not every agenda slide does this efficiently, nor does every presentation call for it. Don't spend 3 minutes of your 15-minute conference presentation talking about what you are *going* to talk about; just get to it. There is no harm *saying* what you are going to talk about—not everything you say needs to go on a slide.

Header Slide. If you used the presentation worksheet at the beginning of this chapter, your presentation is already broken up into several sections. As you move through your presentation, you can give your audience guideposts as sections begin and end to help them follow your argument. I call these "header" slides because they help your audience get a sense of where you are headed.

Photo by Ludovic Charlet on Unsplash.

Breaker Slide. A breaker slide is simply a slide with no information on it. It can be black, white, blue, whatever; its purpose is to give your audience a rest and help them focus their attention back on you.

Ending Slide. Far too many concluding slides consist of a simple word or two: "Questions?" or "Thank You!" This is a wasted opportunity; you can always thank your audience verbally, but the slide space should be used to reinforce your conclusion. You've already constructed a concise, active headline in your worksheet, so put it on your last slide. You want people to leave your talk with your concluding statement utmost in their minds.

Photo by Katie Moum on Unsplash.

Giving Your Presentation

While attending the many presentations given in your organization, department, or field's conferences, you have probably seen your fair share of bad ones: overloaded text slides, poor graphs, blurry photographs, speakers who face the screen and repeatedly say, "uh." In other words, the bar is set very low to deliver a great presentation. If you can apply just some of the techniques in this chapter, your presentation will be a marked improvement over how most of your peers present their work.

One of the most important things you can do to give a great presentation is to practice. And practice. And practice some more. You can practice your 15-minute conference presentation four times in an hour. The more you practice, the more familiar you will be with your content, which will ultimately reduce the need for text- and bullet-point-heavy presentations. Practicing moves you away from your natural inclination to include lots of text on your slides.

When you practice, don't mindlessly click through your slides as you sit at your desk mumbling what you plan to say. Turn off your phone, close your email, and shut your door. Stand up, use a slide clicker, and practice your presentation out loud. As you practice, you will find the places where your presentation doesn't hold together or concepts don't flow. You might find that your planned 15-minute talk is taking you 45 minutes.

Try to be confident and enthusiastic when you stand in front of your audience. It's okay to be nervous-even experienced presenters get nervous—but if your nerves or discomfort are visible, your audience will pick it up. There's little reason for an audience member to be excited about your content if you're not excited about it. There are lots of things you can do to alleviate anxiety and nervousness: try exercise, meditation, or deep breathing. It's also useful to arrive early. That way, you can get your computer, notes, and other materials and technology set up. I find it valuable to have a checklist of technical and other things I need to bring with me, which is why I've created a *Presentation Supplies Checklist* that you can find at the end of this chapter and an editable version on the book's website.

Wrapping Up

As you prepare your next presentation, this time don't hurry to your computer, boot up your presentation software, and start typing. Instead, think carefully about your message and how you want to share your information, and plan your talk accordingly.

Everything you put on your slides should have a purpose. Try to follow these guidelines:

- **Visualize** your content, from the dense table of statistics to the header slides that help you transition from one section to another. Your audience is much more likely to recognize and remember your content if you present it visually.
- **Unify** what you say with what you show. Be consistent across your slide design and your presentation style. Doing so will reduce the amount of mental energy your audience will spend as you move from one slide or section to the next. The result will be an audience that spends more time engaging with you, your content, and your message.

- **Focus** your audience's attention on each point, each number, and each fact you want them to take away. You don't need to present them with everything at once. Control what they see and when they see it by focusing their attention where you want it.

A presentation is a fundamentally different form of communication than what you write down and publish in a journal, report, or blog post. Bring your audience along with you on the journey of your presentation, so they will remember you and your presentation and act on the content you deliver.

Key Takeaways

- Be an audience-centric speaker rather than a presenter-centric speaker. Consider how your presentation is going to help your audience and make your design and presentation decisions with your audience in mind.
- Plan and practice your presentation. You spend weeks or months on the written project; spend a few hours on your presentation.
- Highlight your most important findings and make sure your audience focuses on them; don't put everything from your report in your presentation. Remember, a presentation is a fundamentally different form of communication.
- Simplify your slides and make them more visual; your audience is more likely to remember and recall more visual information.

Presentation Books

Michael Alley. In *The Craft of Scientific Presentations*, Alley lays out a particular approach to scientific presentation delivery and includes a long list of scientific evidence for his approach from the psychology, neuroscience, and education fields.

Matt Carter. One of the few specialized books on this subject, Carter's *Designing Science Presentations* provides good insight on how to present scientific information in various formats.

Nancy Duarte. Author of several books on presentation skills and design including *Slide:ology*, *Resonate*, and *Data Story*, Duarte's books are modern classics in the presentation field. Her books primarily focus on how to create better slides and give better presentations.

Carmine Gallo. Gallo's book, *The Presentation Secrets of Steve Jobs* dissects the Apple co-founder's presentations. He shows how Jobs' approach and design are effective ways to present information, and he describes how they can be applied to improve your work. In *Talk Like TED*, Gallo breaks down the strategy involved for hundreds of successful TED talks. His latest book, *The Storyteller's Secret*, covers the storytelling strategies of business leaders and speakers.

Garr Reynolds. Author of modern classics *Presentation Zen*, *Presentation Zen: Design*, and *The Naked Presenter*, Reynolds's books focus on basic presentation skills and design. He is a proponent of simple, clean slides that more effectively present information with before-and-after examples.

Jonathan Schwabish. My own book, *Better Presentations: a Guide for Researchers, Scholars, and Wonks*, is designed for presenters of scholarly or data-intensive content. It details essential strategies for developing clear, sophisticated, and visually captivating presentations and presents the information from this chapter in more detail.

Echo Swinford and **Julie Terberg.** Their *Building PowerPoint Templates* is probably the best book on creating themes and templates in PowerPoint. It teaches you to build presentations with consistent branding and design that can be shared between collaborators or across an organization.

Robin Williams. Author of *The Non-Designer's Design Book*, a primer on design, Williams provides a perfect text for those needing an introduction to color, font, layout, and other aspects of design.

Design Resources

Below are some suggestions for both free and for-pay resources to find good photographs, icons, and fonts. These resources and websites are always changing, and new tools and sites are constantly emerging.

Photography

iStockPhoto, Shutterstock, and Corbis Images. These are just three of the many for-pay photo sites available on the Internet, each of which has different subscription and purchase options. Be aware that some of these sites may have different licensing agreements for different uses (e.g., use in a book versus in a blog post).

Flickr Creative Commons. This is a photo-posting and sharing site with millions of users around the world. By default, many of these photos are available for free and for use through Creative Commons, a global nonprofit organization that helps enable sharing and licensing of creative content around the world.

Unsplash. Images you find on Unsplash can be used for free and without attribution for both personal and commercial use, making it a terrific resource if you don't have a budget for purchasing photos. Other good websites that provide completely free images are Pexels, Pixabay, Gratisography, and Little Visuals.

Icons

Iconmnstr. This site hosts more than 3,000 high-quality icons, all free for use with no attribution required.

Noun Project. This is an online community of designers who contribute their own icons to the library. There are different download and purchasing options available. You can download icons for free as long as you attribute the designer, or you can purchase icons for under $5.

PowerPoint. The newest versions of PowerPoint include a built-in library of icons that you can insert and edit directly in your slides.

Fonts

Font Squirrel Some fonts on this site are free, and some are available for purchase. The site shows you all the different fonts within a family (e.g., regular, bold, and thin), is clear about the licensing, and explains how to download the files.

Google Fonts. This no-frills site from Google has hundreds of free fonts, which you can browse with simple search and drop-down menus. Google Fonts may be your best bet when looking for free fonts. Google also allows you to enter your own text to test how it will appear in a presentation.

Presentation Worksheet

Presentation Title

1. **What type of presentation are you giving?**

   ❏ Small meeting
   ❏ Department or conference seminar
   ❏ Classroom lecture
   ❏ Sales pitch/funding request
   ❏ Keynote address
   ❏ Workshop
   ❏ Other

2. **Who is your audience?**

   ❏ Coworkers or colleagues
   ❏ Managers
   ❏ Scientists/technical professionals
   ❏ Salespeople and marketers
   ❏ Students
   ❏ Mixed
   ❏ Other

3. **What is the headline message of your presentation?**

4. **What do you want your audience to do with your conclusions?**

5. **Craft your opening statement.**

6. **Craft your closing statement.**

7. **Outline the sections of your presentation.**
    1.
    2.
    3.
    4.
    5.

8. **What stories can you tell?**

9. **Images (sketch or describe before searching)**
    ❑ Graphs and charts
    ❑ Pictures, illustrations, and icons
    ❑ Videos

10. **Anticipated Q&A**
    1. Q:
        A:
    2. Q:
        A:

Presentation Preparation Checklist

Logistics to arrange with host

❑ Audience type and goals

❑ Number in audience

❑ Transportation to/from location

❑ Start and end times

❑ Audio/visual requirements

❑ Length and frequency of breaks and meals

❑ Any cultural events to account for (e.g., prayer times)

❑ Who is introducing and for how long

❑ Webinar platform

❑ Sharing slides and fonts

❑ Length of expected Q&A

Gear

❑ Computer, charger, and extension cord

❑ Projector adapters and extension cords

❑ Presentation clicker

❑ Batteries

❑ Portable speaker

❑ USB drive with presentation backup

❑ Dry erase markers or chalk

❑ Food, water, throate lozenges, etc.

❑ Microphone (if not provided by host)

Reminders

❑ Turn off or silence phone

❑ Remove unnecessary objects from pockets (e.g., keys)

❑ Make microphone comfortable

❑ Check clothes and hair

❑ Relax, breathe, or meditate

Case Study: *Using the power of storytelling to communicate your message*

Telling the story of how data is transforming lives in three underserved communities, Urban Institute researchers were able to bring their work to life for new audiences.

Promise Neighborhoods, a federal initiative inspired by the Harlem Children's Zone, strives to end intergenerational poverty in low-income communities by supporting children from birth to college. Urban Institute researchers provide technical assistance on data collection to Promise Neighborhood grantees across the country. The initiative's reliance on data to guide each site's interventions is what sets Promise Neighborhoods apart from many previous antipoverty initiatives, and it's what ensures that children and families get the tailored support they need.

To help grantees in this effort, Urban provides guidance on data collection, performance measurement, and performance management. This work is crucial, but its impact is not always well understood—and it can be hard to engage and excite audiences by talking about technical assistance. We knew that the best way to tell the story of how performance data is making a difference was to tell the story of how children, families, and neighborhoods on the receiving end were benefiting.

To do that, Urban's communications team reported, wrote, and photographed stories about three Promise Neighborhood grantees: one aiming to close the disparity of opportunities in rural Indianola, Mississippi; another working to lift an isolated and forgotten Washington, DC, community out of poverty; and

(continued)

a third striving to meet the needs of families from San Francisco's gentrifying Mission District, even as many residents were being displaced.

The stories grounded Urban's technical work in the initiative's ultimate goal: helping children thrive and succeed. By illustrating how grantees used data to map the landscape of needs, connect families to vital services, and figure out what's working and what's not, the stories made the abstract idea of a "data-driven, place-based" initiative concrete and relatable. They showed why data matters and opened up Urban's work to new audiences who may not have been drawn to our more technical research reports.

Feature stories and blog posts are natural platforms for storytelling. To put our data on long prison terms in perspective, for example, we interviewed men and women who had been incarcerated for over 20 years. To illustrate our data on how far students travel to school in cities that have expanded school choice options, we followed one DC student and her grand-mother as they drove over an hour to school during morning rush hour traffic.

The story you tell can also be your story—what you experi-enced firsthand at a site visit or a conference, how you solved a difficult problem, or why you care about a particular issues or field of research.

Storytelling is a powerful form of connection and communi-cation. Urban stories have put readers in the shoes of unem-ployed workers struggling to get back on their feet, homeless youth trying to navigate city supports, and Native American families reconnecting with cultural traditions. These stories have illustrated our research findings and put a voice and face to the issues we study.

chapter five

How to Blog about Your Findings

Nicole Levins

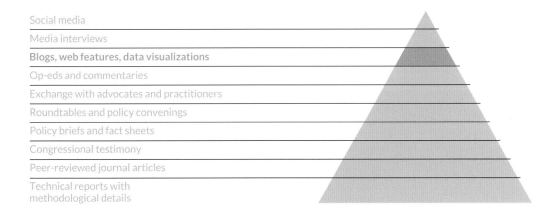

I will be honest with you, I am not going to read a 75-page report.
—Senior Counsel, U.S. House of Representatives
(National Journal 2018)

Why do you conduct research? To satisfy personal or intellectual curiosity? To acquire fame and fortune? To get tenure? For many researchers, their ultimate aim is to influence decision-making or help inform public policy. To that end, it's unlikely that busy policy-makers or thought leaders are going to read your 75-page research paper packed with equations and appendices. If that's the case, how do you get your message into the hands of those who can use it to make better policy decisions?

Meaty, in-depth research products will always have a place in pro-fessional communications. In fact, as discussed in the introduction and illustrated at the beginning of each chapter, those reports are the foundation for all your outreach. By distilling and repackaging the message, you can make your work more appealing to and digest-ible for broader audiences. In this chapter, you'll learn why blogging matters for communicating research, and what you need to know to get started.

What Is a Blog?

A blog ("weblog"; noun, *archaic*) is an online publication, updated regularly by one or more authors, or "bloggers." What a blog covers depends on the blogger(s); it can be a source of original reporting and analysis, opinions, or personal musings on any topic of interest.

Some blogs are affiliated with major news organizations; the *ABC News' FiveThirtyEight* and the *New York Times*'s The Upshot both fea-ture posts on various themes written by multiple reporters. Other blogs are run by individuals, businesses, schools, and nonprofits.

Thanks to free, personal blogging platforms like Blogger, Tumblr, and WordPress, anyone can start a blog—and millions of people have. As of December 2019, Tumblr alone had more than 480 million blogs on its platform.

A blog post is an individual piece of content published on a blog, usually written in a conversational tone and clocking in at just a few hundred words. Most blog posts are text-based and look like articles you'd find in a news publication, but some posts may include multimedia elements such as photos, videos, or audio.

Though "blog" and "blog post" are often used interchangeably, they shouldn't be. If you say, "I'm writing a blog on my new report," you're saying that you're writing what amounts to an entire online publication about your report. What you probably mean is, "I'm writing a single blog post on my new report."

Why Should I Blog?

You spent weeks, months, or even years conducting your research. You spent hours upon hours writing an in-depth research report explaining your methodology and highlighting your findings. Now you need to spend hours writing something else (sorry).

A blog post will likely be a lighter lift than a research report, but it can still be a major time commitment. But done right, the payoff can be enormous.

At its core, blogging is important because more people will learn about your work—and actually read it. A 10- or 20-page document can still intimidate some readers, even those already engaged in your subject. A blog post's shorter length and more accessible language offers a lower psychological barrier to entry. Many readers will get what they need from a blog post, but some will want to go deeper into the research, and the full report will only be a click away.

Blogging also allows you to connect with important stakeholders like peers, policymakers, and the media. Publishing a new blog post on your findings gives you an excuse to reach out to your contacts and update them on what you're working on. This might also help you position yourself front-of-mind for a funding opportunity or a media or job interview. It's also great fodder for your social media accounts (see Chapter 7).

Creating and maintaining a blog also helps you build your personal brand. I suspect the most universally well-known researchers churn out tweets and LinkedIn updates, give frequent interviews, and have a well-designed and regularly updated website, even if they're not prolifically publishing new research. In other words, they have a strong personal brands.

Pokémon GO

In 2016 during the height of the Pokémon GO mania, two Urban Institute researchers used the mobile game's ubiquity as an opportunity to talk about their work in the place-making space. Their accessible, straightforward, and engaging data analysis showed that those living in disadvantaged neighborhoods were largely excluded from participating in the global phenomenon. The resulting blog post garnered coverage in major media outlets and launched an important discussion about inclusivity and urban life.

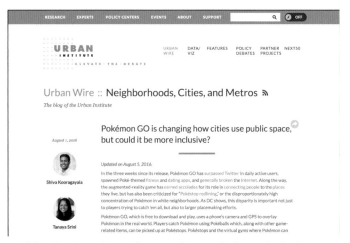

Source: Urban Institute, https://www.urban.org/urban-wire/pokemon-go
-changing-how-cities-use-public-space-could-it-be-more-inclusive.

Even if you're not tapping into a new trend or phenomenon, done right, a blog post can drive conversation about your work for years to come. In 2013, two researchers wrote a blog post about evidence-based ways to reduce crime. Titled simply "Five ways to reduce crime," the post briefly summarized and linked to five Urban Institute research products. To date, the post has received tens of thousands of page views, and it continues to drive traffic to those other research reports.

Source: Urban Institute, https://www.urban.org/urban-wire/five-ways -reduce-crime.

Maintaining a personal blog or regularly contributing to a well-trafficked blog helps position you as an expert. At the Urban Institute, researchers' blog posts are frequently referenced and linked to in major media publications.

How Do I Blog about My Research?

Think about a congressional staffer, nonprofit advocate, or a high-level decisionmaker glancing at his phone, maybe standing on the bus on the way to the office, checking in between meetings, or scrolling through the news over coffee—crunched for time, and expected to know a lot of things about a lot of topics. What do *you* want them to know? What's the best way to reach him?

Coming Up with a Concept

A blog post is a complement to your longer, more in-depth report. A blog post is *not* a press release, an executive summary, or a shorter version of your paper. A blog post must be able to stand alone. For those who've read the research, a blog post should offer a fresh angle; for those who haven't, it should entice them to want to seek more information. Either way, readers should come away from your post having learned something new.

Writing about your research without explicitly writing the full treatment of your research is far less limiting than you might think. Use your research as a jumping-off point to explore a different angle.

- **Share your unique perspective.** What can you offer on this topic that no one else can? Maybe you worked closely with community members, have on-the-ground experience in the field, or worked with an exciting new dataset. Or maybe this work affects you or your community personally. Although you don't have to write a confessional piece, a little humanity is always welcome.

- **Surprise your readers.** What would people be surprised to learn about this topic? What surprised *you*?

- **Highlight next steps.** Even if your paper is 50 pages long, you probably didn't get to everything you wanted to say. What came up in your work that you'd like to explore more? Is it indicative of a larger trend? You could even ask readers to share their thoughts, ideas, and suggestions.

- **Identify a hook.** Are related policy discussions happening in your organization, city, across the country, or around the world? Can your work shed new light on major news events? Capitalize on and add to those existing conversations.

Don't try to do too much, and definitely don't try to hit all of these angles at once. Limit yourself to one point per post instead of trying to pack in every finding and nuance in your work. Have multiple points to make? Great—you've figured out your next few posts.

What Should My Post Sound Like?

Your blog post should be written in an accessible, straightforward tone. Think about how you'd explain your work to a friend or family member. Would you open with a detailed explanation of your methodology? Use a ton of jargon or acronyms? Cram as many $10 words as you can in a single sentence? Probably not. Save the SAT vocabulary for the report, and post like you're having a conversation with someone.

The first sentences—really, the first three words—of your post are make-or-break. Your readers will decide within seconds whether they want to continue. Open with a compelling statistic or quote. Write in the first person, and in the active voice; include a short anecdote or story.

It doesn't have to be formal. You might tell a story about why you became interested in this research, or about a surprise that came up in the process. Use this opportunity to connect with your audience in a more personal way that you might not be able to do in your formal report or journal article.

Whatever you do, don't bury your main point under a 500-word introduction or save it for your conclusion. You're not building a sense of mystery; you're just losing your readers.

Some researchers and academics worry that writing at a "lower grade level" detracts from their credibility. I can't promise you won't be judged by some out-of-touch colleagues, but when your ideas are reaching and resonating with the audiences that matter to you, will you care? I'm not telling you to "dumb down" your content or try to reach the "lay reader." I'm urging you to trim the excess and hone your writing for the blog-reading audience.

Stripping out the jargon and writing in a clear voice does not mean being less sophisticated. The work of some universally regarded "best" writers clocks in at a middle-school level. Where would you rank Ernest Hemingway's *The Old Man and the Sea*? If you guessed grade 8, you're way too high. On the Flesch-Kincaid Grade Level test—a standard test that measures the difficulty of a passage to understand—Hemingway's book scores a 4. Believe it or not, this chapter is a 7.4.

Hemingway's low score stems from the concept of fluency. In a 2015 blog post, strategist Shane Snow explains:

> "Fluency" means the reader can get through the writing quickly, without having to think so hard about the words themselves. My reading level data verifies that Hemingway et al. write with more fluency than others. That's what makes them exceptional. And it gives them a better chance to reach larger audiences.

If you use Microsoft Word, you can check your own readability using Word's internal tool (enable the "Show readability statistics" function under proofing options). Don't stress about hitting a certain grade level, but if your blog posts consistently rank above grade 9 and you're not happy with your web traffic or the feedback you've received, it might be worth rethinking your approach. A high grade may be perfectly appropriate for your formal report or journal article, but it may be less appropriate for the readers of your blog.

Before you swing too far in the opposite direction, remember that blogging is not an excuse to unleash your inner novelist. Sure, readers want to be entertained and engaged, but they also have other things to do. Deliver your message as quickly, directly, and efficiently as possible. Always keep your target audience in mind—that policymaker or practitioner with five minutes to skim through her feed before she's on to the next thing.

At Urban, I occasionally edit content on workforce development. My mother works as a job counselor for a local workforce development agency. She doesn't conduct academic research, but she's well versed in the tissue and the on-the-ground implications of policy changes. When I'm reviewing a post about the Workforce Investment and Opportunity Act or one-stop career centers, I ask myself if my mom would want to read it. Would it make sense to her? Is it useful? Would she share it with her coworkers? If time permits, I'll ask her directly.

If it helps, identify your own version of my mom.

What Should My Blog Post Look Like?

There are four basic elements to a standard blog post.

1. **Title.** The title is probably the most important part of your post. It's how you hook your readers, and it's likely how they're finding your content in the first place (via social media or web search). Which is more appealing: "Keep your footage out of your mouth: Why 'public' shouldn't mean 'public' when it comes to accessing police body-camera footage" or "Police body-camera footage: Why 'public' should only kind of mean 'public'"? The first includes a terrible pun, obscures what the post is about, and is very long, with nearly twice as many words as the second.

   The best titles are a mix of declaration and intrigue. Some tips:

   - **Take a headline approach.** Don't hide the payoff. If your post will teach readers four things they should know about a new housing bill, tell them that in the title. You should also make it social media friendly. In other words, your title should be concise and active. Readers are more likely to share your content with their networks if they don't have to think too much about what their social media post should say.

   - **Keep it short.** Google search results only display about the first 70 characters of a title, according to a late 2017 report by Internet marketing company Big Leap.

   - **Make it search-friendly.** What words and phrases do people use when they're looking for information on your topic? What are you seeing in the news or on social media, or what are you hearing from others in your space? Really understanding search-engine optimization (SEO) is not for the faint of heart, but there are lots of good tools you can use if you're interested. For example, Google's keyword planner (https://ads.google.com/home/tools/keyword-planner/) lets you explore how many monthly searches certain keywords and phrases receive.

- **Avoid clichés.** Stand-alone generic phrases like "Follow the money," "Think outside the box," or "Get the ball rolling" don't tell your potential readers—or search engines—what's in store. Same thing with puns—sure, they're fun, but if they obscure what your post is about, your potential readers won't be able to find it. If you've come up with a pun that's too clever to waste, consider adding a colon and more descriptive words—for example, the book *Game of Loans: The Rhetoric and Reality of Student Debt*—but keep an eye on the total character length.

  If you're struggling with a title, I suspect you're also struggling with what you're trying to say in your post. Really think about that single, definitive point you want to make. Make sure your title you post supports that point, and delete the rest. From there, coming up with a title will be much easier.

2. **Subheads and bullets.** Like it or not, few readers are going to make it through every word of your post. Anticipate scanning, and do what you can to help those busy readers get what they need.

   - **Consider subheads if your post has more than one distinct section.** If you're writing about the renewal of a bill in Congress, for example, you might want to include some brief background on its initial passage. Identifying one section as "Some history on H.B. 123" and another as "What's happening with H.B. 123 today" lets those who are more familiar with the topic skip right to part two, while those who are new get brought up to speed.

   - **Bullets are the ultimate shortcut.** Break out and list your individual thoughts. How much easier has it been to get through these bulleted sections? Although bulleted lists might not work in your 25-page academic journal article, they're helpful to blog readers.

- **Try numbered lists.** It's gotten a bad rap thanks to clickbait pieces like "21 things all '90s kids know—the answers might surprise you!" but the numbered list is a popular and effective blog post format. If it makes sense to do so, try framing your post as "10 (or fewer) things you need to know about X." It lets readers know what they're signing up for—"I have time to make it through 6 things"—and what the payoff will be—"today I will learn 6 things about federal health-care reform."

3. **Multimedia.** To really engage your audience, go beyond text and include visuals.

   - **Photos.** Can you use photos, illustrations, or icons to help give your topic a visual hook? Have you taken your own photos related to your work? There are lots of great websites and resources for images, including Shutterstock, iStockPhoto, Flickr, and The Noun Project (see the box at the end of Chapter 4). Be sure to double-check the copyright permissions for anything you download or purchase; photos are nice to have, but they're not worth a lawsuit.

   - **Video.** Have you or your organization created a video that sums up or supports your post? Are you featured in a related news clip? Did you speak at a conference or on a panel? You can directly post the video along with your blog post or, if the video is posted to another site such as YouTube, you can usually embed it right in your blog post (by using what is called an "embed code," which you can copy and paste).

   - **Graphs.** Can you adapt some visuals from your research, or crunch numbers from another data source? Simple charts with compelling titles, some helpful annotations, and, if applicable, a logo to credit the source, help drive home your most powerful points. Take a look at the following example, which appeared in a blog post on visibility for women of color. This stark illustration of the wealth gaps people of color face is much more striking than a single sentence (see Chapter 3 for more on effective data visualization techniques).

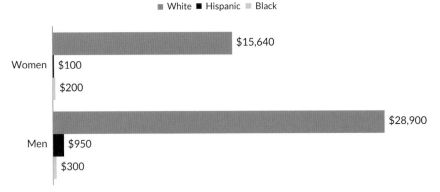

Median Wealth for Single Men and Single Women by Race/Ethnicity, Ages 18–64

■ White ■ Hispanic ■ Black

Women
$15,640
$100
$200

Men
$28,900
$950
$300

Source: Mariko Chang, "Women and Wealth: Insights for Grantmakers" (Washington, DC: Asset Funders Network, n.d.).

Source: Urban Institute, https://www.urban.org/urban-wire/visibility-women -color-crucial-first-step-toward-equality.

4. **Links.** Links serve two roles in a blog post: shortcuts and citations. Rather than wasting 300 words defining concepts or providing background information, add links to high-quality, legitimate sources you trust, such as research organizations, academic journals, or news organizations.

   And although your post should be grounded in evidence, you don't need to include footnotes or other formal citations; just add a hyperlink to the full report or other resources. If you'd like to explicitly acknowledge the source, say something like "According to a 2015 Urban Institute report . . ." Don't hyperlink words like *report* and *here*—your links should tell a story. Readers who skim your post often jump from link to link, so add the link to text that also helps highlight the point of the paragraph or passage. Which of the following is more eye-catching?

   • Based on my <u>calculations</u> of 2016 census data, 51 percent of white women are married . . . but only 26 percent of black women and 36 percent of American Indian women are in that position.

- Based on my calculations of 2016 Census data, <u>51 percent of white women are married . . . but only 26 percent of black women and 36 percent of American Indian women</u> are in that position.

How Long Does This Thing Have to Be?

There's no hard and fast rule for word count. For some audiences, longer is fine. Using data from posts published on Medium.com, social media company Buffer identified 1,600 words as "the optimal length for a blog post." Marketing company CoSchedule found 2,500-word posts ranked best for search, and HubSpot came to a similar conclusion.

But those studies looked at broad online audiences. Remember who you're writing for—the CEO, legislative aide, or communications assistant on his or her coffee break—and err on the side of brevity. Even if you're writing for a more niche or technical audience, be respectful of your readers' time.

If you're writing for another organization's or individual's platform, ask what works best for their audience or best fits their editorial style. They may have a policy on blog post length; they might also know that their readers tend to drop off after 600 words.

In general, I recommend aiming for 400 to 800 words, which gives you enough space to go fairly deep on a topic without overwhelming readers. Those who want to go even deeper will click through to the research.

Another thing to keep in mind: Keep your paragraphs short—four lines or fewer, if possible. Big blocks of text with no visual breaks can appear overwhelming to digital readers, especially if they're reading on a mobile device. You don't necessarily have to write shorter text; just add a hard return at the end of each unique idea to make your post easier to scan.

Which post would you rather read as you scroll through it on your phone, the one on the left or the one on the right?

Today, the federal prison population is 750 percent bigger than it was in 1980, costing taxpayers billions of dollars and making no measurable impact on public safety. What factors are driving this growth? What can be done to stem the tide? To come up with answers, Congress created the Charles Colson Task Force on Federal Corrections. The bipartisan team will examine challenges in the federal corrections system and develop practical, data-driven policy responses. At the end of the year, members will present their findings and recommendations to Congress, the Department of Justice, and the president. The Urban Institute is providing research, analysis, strategic guidance, and logistical support in partnership with the Center for Effective Public Policy through a cooperative agreement with the Bureau of Justice Assistance.

Today, the federal prison population is 750 percent bigger than it was in 1980, costing taxpayers billions of dollars and making no measurable impact on public safety. What factors are driving this growth? What can be done to stem the tide?

To come up with answers, Congress created the Charles Colson Task Force on Federal Corrections. The bipartisan team will examine challenges in the federal corrections system and develop practical, data-driven policy responses.

At the end of the year, members will present their findings and recommendations to Congress, the Department of Justice, and the president.

The Urban Institute is providing research, analysis, strategic guidance, and logistical support in partnership with the Center for Effective Public Policy through a cooperative agreement with the Bureau of Justice Assistance.

Where Do I Publish This Thing? How?

It can be helpful to tap into existing audiences, especially when you're new to blogging. If your organization has a blog, that may be your best place to start. Get in touch with the blog manager or editor. Before you've written a word, find out if what you'd like to write about fits the platform. She might suggest other angles to pursue, share blogging guidelines and details about the process, or connect you with other bloggers at your organization.

Or the blog manager or editor might say, "No, thanks," and you'll have to publish elsewhere. If that's the case, they still might be able to help you on the technical side or give you other tips, pointers, and resources.

If your organization doesn't have a blog or doesn't have space for you, you have other options:

- Do you work with funders, partners, or other organizations with blogs? Ask if they'll give you a guest-blogging spot, or let you team up with one of their staffers for a co-written post. Again, this gives you access to an established audience.
- Some media organizations welcome expert guest posts. Do you or your colleagues have relationships with reporters? Make sure you're well-versed in the content they're looking for and pitch yourself and your work. That first step is very, very important: cold calls are rarely successful, and if they're tone deaf or totally off base, you're definitely not setting yourself up for a win (see the next chapter for more on working with reporters).

If writing for another organization doesn't work, or if you'd prefer to set off on your own, a plethora of free or low-cost, user-friendly blogging platforms allow anyone to create his own publication (see the box on the next page, *A Few of Today's Top Blogging Platforms*). You don't need to be a web designer or know code to launch a blog; simply visit these sites, click the sign-up button, and walk through the steps. Congrats: you now have a blog and all the responsibilities that go along with it.

Among those options, my top recommendation. In some ways, it's more reminiscent of a social network than a blogging platform, and it's more conducive to sharing and community. And if you're not convinced, you can post regularly or infrequently; if you really only want to publish a one-off post, Medium is much more forgiving.

Though LinkedIn is a social media network, not technically a blogging platform, it's expanding more into publishing and can be a valuable outlet, especially for those who already have a robust presence on the site. Like Medium, LinkedIn is also a good place for one-off or irregular or infrequent posts (also see Chapter 7).

A Few of Today's Top Blogging Platforms

If this book had been written in 2011, a platform called Posterous would be on this list but the company folded in 2013. That's a roundabout way of saying these recommendations are subject to change.

Blogger. You might remember the deluge of user.blogspot.com blogs in the early 2000s. Now a part of Google's suite of personal digital tools, it offers all the basic features necessary to launch an entry-level blog (though it lacks the pizazz of other Google products).

LinkedIn. This is a social network for professionals, mostly used for professional networking. It is also a place to publish "articles" on your work, your field, or whatever your heart desires without the responsibility of maintaining a separate blog.

Medium. A place for "social journalism," where amateur bloggers mix with established writers and publications—and where an unknown author with a compelling post could make a major splash. This happened in early 2016 when Talia Jane published "An Open Letter to My CEO," which detailed the financial struggles she faced as an employee at Yelp and sparked a global conversation about employment and entitlement.

Tumblr. This is a blogging platform with a social media slant. In addition to posting original content, ranging from traditional blog posts to wordless graphic interchange formats (GIFs), users follow, share ("reblog"), and engage with others' content. The audience tends to skew younger: one source estimates that 66 percent of its users are under age 35.

> **WordPress.** This is one of the most popular content management systems on the Internet today. The company claims that nearly one-third of the web, from major news sites to personal blogs, relies on its platform. Like Blogger, it offers a simple and fairly straightforward interface, though more advanced users can experiment with various plugins, templates, and other customizations.

I Blogged! Now What?

Just because you built/blogged it doesn't mean the readers will come. It's up to you to get the word out. What communications channels can you tap into? Organizational newsletters, personal email outreach, your organization's social media accounts, and your personal social media accounts are all great resources. Use the other strategies you're learning in this book to drive readers to your work.

How can you tell whether blogging was worth the effort? The number of page views and site visitors isn't the only metric. Qualitative wins are just as valuable as quantitative ones—if not more. Did your post receive thoughtful comments? Did someone in your field see your post and send you a note? Did your post gain traction on social media? Did it appeal to a funder? Were you quoted in the media as a result of its publication? How you measure your success is up to you.

You also don't have to go it alone. Build relationships with fellow bloggers and bounce ideas off one another. Ask a trusted colleague or friend to review your drafts. Ask someone whose work you admire to co-author a piece. Connect with other bloggers to see if you could share content across your platforms, helping you to reach wider audiences.

Remember, 10 page hits from the right people can be more important than 1,000 hits from random people on the Internet. Regardless of what success means to you, don't get discouraged if you don't achieve it right away—because you probably won't. Keep trying, and keep trying new approaches. You'll only get better at blogging, and blogging will only get easier.

Key Takeaways

- Blogging expands your audience—and your impact. Blogging can be an effective way to get your research out into the world and into the hands of people who can turn your findings into action.

- Keep your posts short and snappy. Remember, one point per post—more than one point means more than one post—and try to make it a quick read. Use links and multimedia as shortcuts.

- Get the word out. Use other communications tools at your disposal to drive readers to your posts.

- Keep trying. Learn from your missteps and celebrate your successes.

Case Study: *Writing timely and accessible blog posts*

For many researchers, blogging is a completely new way of writing. While some are wary of using a news hook and a few hundred words as entry points to a complex research product, others have embraced this approach and seen its benefits.

Heather Hahn, a senior fellow in the Center for Labor, Human Services, and Population at the Urban Institute, studies the well-being of children and families. As a regular contributor to Urban's blog, *Urban Wire*, she has developed a strong understanding of what makes an effective blog post by working closely with Urban's communications team.

In October 2017, Hahn and other Urban researchers were planning to release their annual *Kids' Share* report, which looks at how much the federal government spends on children. Hahn realized Halloween could be an effective hook for a blog post about the report, so she asked Robert Abare, the *Urban Wire* editor, to help her connect the holiday and the report.

Doing a little digging, Abare found that Americans spend about $9 billion on Halloween each year. That number mirrored a finding in the *Kids' Share* report that the federal government spends about $9 billion a year on the Head Start program, which supports the educational development of children from low-income households.

Hahn worked with Abare to develop the post, which uses that one fact—*Americans spend as much on Halloween as the federal government spends on Head Start*—to draw readers' interest to the broader *Kids' Share* report. The simple comparison made the research finding accessible and easier to put into perspective. Her post highlighted the report's takeaway that federal

(continued)

spending on children is shrinking. And she did it all in less than 300 words.

The post was published on Halloween 2017, leveraging a timely hook to drive engagement. It was widely shared on social media and quickly received over 1,000 page views.

Hahn's blog post shows how to focus on one clear point and use a news hook to attract readers and interest them in a larger body of work. Urban Institute communications staff often point to this example when advising researchers how to write short, snappy blog posts that are timely, shareable, and easy for a broad audience to understand.

chapter six

Working with the Media to Increase Your Impact

Stu Kantor

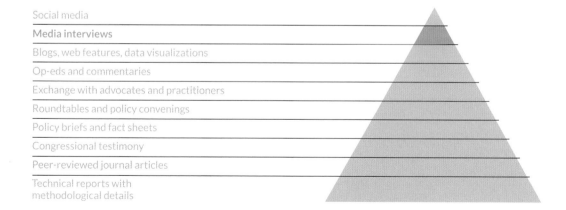

Social media

Media interviews

Blogs, web features, data visualizations

Op-eds and commentaries

Exchange with advocates and practitioners

Roundtables and policy convenings

Policy briefs and fact sheets

Congressional testimony

Peer-reviewed journal articles

Technical reports with methodological details

Moving up the communications pyramid, we now arrive at conducting interviews with the media. Many people are nervous when speaking to reporters, thinking that they are going to be misrepresented, misquoted, or misunderstood. The truth is, reporters and researchers are often working toward the same goal: improving lives through the creation and communication of knowledge. Both groups want to contribute to a more informed public and to better policies, programs and procedures.

Researchers and reporters go about their business—often spoken about proudly as public-service missions—in many common ways. They ask questions, test and revise hypotheses, gather data (quantitative and qualitative) from primary and secondary sources, draw conclusions, discuss implications, offer recommendations, and highlight promising solutions. Although both groups may share the same goals, they approach them from different directions.

This chapter explores the relationship between the researcher and reporter, and how you can effectively cultivate this connections to help your work find its way into the hands of people who can use and benefit from it. The lessons shared here are not exclusively useful for media interviews, however. Although you may not speak to the media, you likely present your work to colleagues and managers. In these cases, some of the strategies and techniques presented in this chapter will be useful as you communicate your work and seek buy-in and approval from those important groups.

Understanding the Media Landscape and the "Why" of Good Media Relations

The media comes in a variety of flavors: print outlets, such as newspapers and magazines; electronic operations, such as radio stations and broadcast and cable television channels; online news and information sites, podcasts, and blogs; wire services, such as the Associated Press; and syndication services, like the *Washington Post News Service* and Syndicate. Some seek national or international readers, listeners, and viewers, whereas others have their eyes on a particular region or state. Some work on behalf of their nearby communities and neighbors.

Another dimension pertains to the audience: many reporters at general-interest organizations, such as the *New York Times* or the

Dallas Morning News, seek to connect with readers who have broad arrays of interests and needs. Others report for subject-specific outlets that cover a particular issue, sector, or profession.

Even with all this variety, building and cultivating a relationship with members of the media involves tried-and-true steps and techniques. Like a solid partnership, it takes diligence and devotion from both sides to get it right, but the rewards make the effort more than worthwhile.

Why help a reporter? A most selfish reason is that the media spotlight can bring your findings and wisdom to the attention of millions of people. A single Associated Press story can be picked up by hundreds of outlets near and far. A story in the *New York Times*, *Washington Post*, or *Wall Street Journal* might prompt local reporters to ask, "How does this situation or problem play out for folks in my state or city?" Media coverage can advance your professional and personal standing and add desirable credibility to your résumé. It can also help you connect with fellow experts, funders, new datasets, and unexpected opportunities.

Media engagement is integral to a researcher's public-service mission and is a powerful means of public education. The CVs of renowned scholars and those who aspire to be leaders in their fields deliberately bring attention to their media appearances. And positive reporting of your findings can add luster to your institution's reputation.

Still, there are reasons you might shy away from media requests. They don't always arrive at an opportune moment. You might worry a reporter will misrepresent or misquote you. Perhaps you're concerned about time. What on the surface might appear to be a simple request could turn into an unexpectedly extended give-and-take between you and the reporter. You might fear you'll get stuck educating a reporter new to a beat or issue, walking her through the basic ins and outs of a topic you have spent years researching.

Yes, these all happen. On a handful of occasions, a research colleague has complained to me that they spent a half hour with a reporter "and all they printed was one sentence from me" or "they completely missed the nuance of my findings." As you'll learn, miscues, blunders, mistakes, and misstatements can be reduced, but there's no guarantee that all your interactions with the news media will come out to your liking. We are, after all, talking about humans, who, even with the best of intentions, have been known to err or disappoint. But, as you can see in the selected quotes shown below, your interactions with reporters can have notable effects on helping to distribute your work to a wider audience.

> "A rising tide is lifting all boats as our country is doing better, but some a lot more than others," said Signe-Mary McKernan, a senior fellow at the Urban Institute and co-director of the institute's opportunity and ownership initiative. "Black and Hispanic families are not on the same wealth building paths as white families."
>
> — *Washington Post, 2017*

> "I don't think any one change is going to really make a dent in the gun violence problem in the U.S.," said Nancy La Vigne, vice president and director of the Justice Policy Center at the Urban Institute. "It's going to take a combination of efforts, including restricting high power firearms, legislative solutions on people who are misusing firearms, and working in high gun violence communities."
>
> — *Fortune, 2018*

The Goal-Focused Expert

Before you contact a reporter, or a reporter's query ever comes your way, whether it's a cold call, an email, or a request from your institution's media relations office, relax and repeat these words:

> I'm an expert. I've devoted much of my professional life to the topic. I know my research. I know the research produced by others in the field. I want people to benefit from what I've found and know.

Reporters want and seek your assistance and insights because *you're an expert*. You may have come to their attention because of a Google search, a referral from another researcher, a tip from the reporter at the next desk over, or because you initiated contact. From the get-go, you have considerable cachet and can, with practice, drive much of the conversation.

Bear in mind, almost all (if not all) the questions reporters pose are information- or insight-seeking. They are not out to get you; they're out to get your wisdom. Reporters want to better understand the issue and need your help illuminating it for their readers, who likely do not share your expertise. In the rare instance when a problematic question is posed, there are techniques to turn it to your advantage.

The most important part of the interview occurs before you pick up the phone, send the email, or walk into the studio. Reporters are busy and overextended—sound familiar?—and often are in search of the concise, punchy, even poetic quote or sound bite that quickly gets to the point and crystallizes a key theme or dimension of their story. They are also looking for real-world examples, even hypothetical ones, that resonate, that illuminate the human condition, that tell a story, and that will make what you're saying real for people.

To make the most of press opportunities, know what you want reporters and the public to know, and know how to tell it. What are *your* goals? You can advance those goals by ably handling your side of the dialogue. Similar strategies are important for speaking to colleagues, managers, and funders: How can you best communicate your work so they can find insights, make discoveries, and implement your ideas?

Researcher, Promote Thyself

Any relationship of value and significance requires both parties to commit themselves to open, honest, and sustained communication. Think about your spouse, partner, academic and research associates, and other people central to your well-being and success.

Reporters are your partners in public education, policy and program improvement, and professional advancement and therefore merit serious engagement. We are, after all, talking about media relations—not media speed dating.

For the sake of this discussion, let's assume your college, company, or organization does not have a media relations unit. If that assumption is wrong, contact them and introduce yourself, get on their calendar for their version of *Media Relations 101: How We Do It Here*, and keep them updated on newsworthy work you're doing and expertise you can offer.

If you don't have anyone to be your media relations ally, don't despair. You're smart, dedicated to your field, and motivated to advance. What's more, you're already a media consumer, so you have at least a passing familiarity with some useful news and information outlets and the folks who work there. And media relations done right does not require you to buy equipment, rent a venue, or carve a lot of time out of your day.

To get started, take a page from the environmental movement's "think globally, act locally." Think expansively about the issues, controversies, policies, programs, and questions that you have the expertise to address. Let's say you're an expert on economic development, the role tax incentives might (or might not) have in bringing businesses to your community, and the trade-offs that should be considered when public dollars are at stake.

Next, note the wrangling taking place nearby (or even far away) over the use of tax incentives, proposals being floated by officials or interest groups, statements by significant parties with vested interests, chatter on talk shows, and commentaries in the media.

What's missing from these conversations, exchanges, and accounts? What misinformation is getting inappropriate attention? What should the public and its representatives know to make fact-grounded decisions? And what information and insights, whether from your own research or gleaned from others in your field, are you ready to bring forth?

Make a list of the newspapers, TV stations, radio stations, news bureaus (such as the Associated Press), online outlets, and bloggers that serve your town, state, or region—that you use, respect, and enjoy. If warranted, go wider and consider national news organizations.

Who might write about or report on tax incentives and efforts to lure companies to your town or state? Business reporters are a natural fit, as are reporters who have a geographic area as their beat, cover relevant government entities such as city hall, or report on politics. Columnists who focus on issues in the region should be on your list, too. Even-keeled radio talk shows, especially on public radio stations, are excellent venues for thoughtful, extended conversations.

Reaching Out to a Reporter

So, you know you have something important to contribute (more about interview preparation later in this chapter) and have a solid sense of the right people to approach. What now?

I have found concise emails an effective, efficient means to engage reporters and encourage a mutually beneficial relationship. Other media relations professionals may prefer reaching out with a phone call. Keep in mind that many reporters disdain cold calls because they are disruptive and can consume a fair amount of time, especially if they come near a deadline. Of course, if you have something that is uniquely timely and revealing—something for which a reporter would drop other obligations—then a phone call might be just the thing.

How do you find a reporter's email or phone number? Many outlets include this information in a staff listing or in staff bios. Also, social media accounts (Twitter in particular) are a good place to find contact information.

Your initial email might be something like the following:

> Ms. Jones,
>
> Your story today <insert link to the story> on Anytown's efforts to create a tax incentive package that will encourage XYZ Corp. to open a new plant here was thorough but missed some essential information. Research has shown that this kind of tax package will do A, B, and C, rather than D, E, and F as John Smith contends.
>
> As a professor of economics at Our State Technical University who has studied the pros and cons of incentive packages for more than a decade, I have a deep and independent understanding of the issue's intricacies. For instance, I wrote this <insert link> and this <insert link>.
>
> I believe I can help you and your readers/viewers/listeners to understand better the advantages, disadvantages, and trade-offs that come with economic development proposals.
>
> I'd appreciate the opportunity to chat with you in the hope that my expertise can aid you and your reporting. My calendar is wide open.
>
> Regards,
> Tina Brown

If Ms. Jones's story spurs you to write to her, try to be swift. This will show that she and her reporting are important to you. Still, she might not respond, opting instead to file your note for the next time she reports on something that can benefit from your insights and understanding.

Letters to the editor and commentaries are also ways to engage the media. The former are usually quick responses to news coverage; the latter are tight essays on an issue of current debate or perhaps on issues that you believe *should be* of current debate.

In both cases, before putting pen to paper or keyboard to screen, check the newspaper's website for its submission rules. Word counts differ from paper to paper, but letters are usually in the range of 100 to 200 words and op-eds are in the 750- to 800-word range.

My advice to would-be op-ed writers: Your initial draft should be about 1,000 words. This will allow you or an editor friend to hone your words to the best 750 or so. Also, and many writers get tripped up here, make sure your commentary presents a powerful opinion. Too many submissions have gone nowhere because the piece was nothing more than a polished rendering of a press release or executive summary.

A provocative op-ed in a newspaper will often catch the attention of other media, prompting interview requests, and garner interest on the part of officials and other stakeholders.

> "Most of us have seen the data on the pay gap: Women earn 80 cents on the dollar compared to men, and for black and Latina women, it's 63 cents and 54 cents respectively. But few people realize that the women's wealth gap is far greater than the income gap. And for women of color, it's not a gap, but a chasm."
>
> — Kilolo Kijakazi and Heather McCulloch op-ed in *Slate, 2018*

> "Today, courts are increasingly recognizing that no statutory basis exists for excluding LGBTQ individuals from the rights provided to us all. The ability of millions of Americans to support their families and live with dignity should not need to wait for further congressional action. Congress has already spoken by prohibiting discrimination based on 'sex.'"
>
> — Jenny Yang op-ed in the *Washington Post, 2019*

When a Reporter Comes Your Way

The first question when a media request comes your way is an easy one: Is the topic or issue one you can satisfactorily address? Perhaps you were the fourth author on a study and made a limited, albeit important, contribution to the research. If the topic is not one you command, say so—and try to recommend others who can contribute to the story. You are wasting your time and the reporter's time if you are not going to give her the expertise she needs; you want the reporter and others at her outlet to know you have their best interests in mind.

Reporters, like researchers, are often time-strapped and facing an approaching deadline; it is therefore essential that you get back to the reporter as soon as possible with a response about whether you can help. This does not necessarily mean you drop everything and do the interview right then and there. In fact, you might need to do a little homework or preparation, look through a research paper or two, or find the most up-to-date data. It's one less worry for the reporter if she knows you'll be available at some mutually agreeable time.

If you have concerns about the media outlet, reporter, or topic, check immediately with your public affairs or media relations office before agreeing to an interview. Someone there can likely get the details you want before proceeding. Most reporters will provide some sample questions in advance so you can judge your suitability, but don't expect a reporter to send you all her questions.

If your organization does not have a media relations office, you may need to do your own research about the request. You can look at the news outlet directly on its website or talk to others who have been interviewed; you might also have a pre-interview email exchange with the reporter to see what questions she has in mind. If you are at all uncomfortable, you can recommend other people the reporter can connect with, an indispensable aid to her work.

Another word of warning: Some reporters will try your patience. Some may be new to a subject (or even to journalism) and may ask for or need some hand-holding. Or, they might be steeped in your research domain and have a long list of detailed questions, making many requests for data, documentation, and other details. If your time is limited, let the reporter know so she can carefully select the most important questions and get the most out of the conversation with you. Remember, the relationship between you and a reporter is a two-way street—both of you are seeking to gain something from the interaction, and thus being up front about expectations and needs can help both sides maximize the advantages from the conversation.

If you're not a seasoned media source, don't worry about getting fancy with ground rules or negotiating what can and cannot be quoted. Go into the interview (or pre-interview exchanges) as if everything you say is on the record and anything you say can be quoted and attributed to you. Consider carefully if you have any contractual obligations with your employer, funder, or other partners. You may also be asked about ongoing research that can't be discussed before publication. Bottom line: know what information you can share and what might be off limits.

Conducting the Interview

You're going to do the interview, and the reporter will be calling you at one o'clock. At this point, you pause, take a nice, deep breath, and get things in order. The most important thing you can do is to identify the most important things you want to convey to the reporter: *What are the two or three headlines, findings, or recommendations you want the reporter to report? What are the must-know statistics, evidence, or proofs that undergird your bold statements?*

Practice your responses out loud. We all sound like accomplished actors in our heads, and saying a response aloud can help you refine what and how you say it (see also Chapter 4 on presentations). You might also practice with someone you can trust to provide constructive criticism. Practice again. And again, if warranted. As a colleague observed, "Say what you might say out loud in the shower, over and over—especially your opening. That way, if nerves kick in, you can rely on muscle memory. Your mouth will remember what to say."

Stay focused on your message points—what you want to tell the story's readers, listeners, or viewers—and stay mindful of the reasons for the reporter's request. You can think of these as the headlines of your work. The interview is your opportunity to shine, to bring forth your research prowess and intellectual vigor, so you need not muzzle yourself with only a handful of practiced headlines. If you have more to say, say it. Share your passion for the work you do and use your voice (especially on radio) to bring warmth and energy to an issue. The reporter (and ultimately the audience) will be more engaged if you sound genuinely excited about your own work. Your headlines make sure you bring your most important contributions to the conversation and they're ready for restatement when the opportunity arises, especially if the reporter's questions go offtrack.

When it's your turn to talk, pause to organize, then state your headline or message point, followed by a supporting fact or two. Pauses give you time to find the right words, enable you to introduce a new idea, protect what you've said, and help the reporter take notes. (I find Marian K. Woodall's book *How to Think on Your Feet* a compact must-read for those wanting more information about how to do their best with their side of a conversation.)

The "answer plus a piece of support" method allows you to maintain your poise, professional demeanor, and credibility and to keep your responses concise. One piece of support is a rule of thumb, not a law. Occasions may arise when you need to give more facts. In doing so, it can be important to give a signal to the reporter that you have a set of facts or supporting evidence. Starting your answer with something like, "There are three main reasons for XYZ . . ." can help you organize your thoughts as you speak while preparing the reporter for an extended answer.

More generally, during the interview, you can help yourself and the reporter with such cues or flags as "the main point," "the most important thing," "there are three reasons," "what's important to understand," and "what's really at stake." Using these kinds of phrases can also help the reporter identify a good quote to use in the story. But don't feel obligated to continue speaking if the reporter is silent; remember, it's the reporter's job to get information from you, so let her do her job.

To prevent a longwinded response, apply the brakes by using the essence of the question as your close: "So X, Y, and Z are the main reasons low-income families have an especially tough time making ends meet." It's your interview, so take your time and repeat information if it's warranted.

Interview Pitfalls

Not all interview questions are clear, concise, and neutral. Sometimes, for various reasons, they can be long, complex, confusing, or even negative. In cases where an interview hits a roadblock, you have several options:

1. Ask to have the question repeated. This will give the reporter a second chance to get it right.

2. Ask—then answer—the question you think should have been asked: "I think you're asking whether . . ."

3. Ask for a clarification or a definition: "Poverty is a complex subject. Can you be more specific?" Or, clarify or define a point yourself: "In my research, poverty is . . ."

4. Respond to one aspect of the question and ignore the rest.

5. Respond indirectly—that is, give the explanation first, then follow with the answer. Question: Why is the XYZ study so late? Answer: Research with people is subject to numerous, all-too-human delays, such as illness and family responsibilities. In this case, circumstances beyond anyone's control added three months to the project.

6. Build a bridge between an inappropriate question and an appropriate response. Agree that something within the question is valid, true, or of concern (such as the importance of educational attainment), then move to the greater concern or more important issue you want to talk about (housing discrimination).

7. Don't validate negative or hostile questions by repeating their problematic elements. Offer a response that focuses on the positive.

8. Be strong: "It's wrong to maintain ABC, because 123."

Various additional techniques and tactics are especially helpful when talking with a reporter, or even a manager, funder, or colleague:

Don't speed speak. Talk at a normal pace, pausing here and there to give yourself a chance to think and the reporter a chance to take accurate notes. During lengthy or complicated conversations, periodically ask the reporter if they understand your answers. Like speaking to an audience, slower is better.

Limit specialized and technical language. You do yourself, the reporter, and the audience a service by banishing or limiting jargon, most particularly if the coverage is for interested laypeople. This is when practicing can be the most helpful, especially if you can rehearse with someone who is not an expert in your field; if your parents can understand your explanation of how Medicaid reimbursements work, then you're likely ready for an interview. Jargon-filled responses in interviews with trade or professional media might be satisfactory, but they rarely result elsewhere in something quotable or memorable. When speaking to a manager or colleague, you may feel that technical jargon is appropriate, and in many cases it is. But also consider what your audience will do with the information you are presenting. Maybe they are the gatekeepers to the next level in the organization or broader group, who may not need all the technical details and statistical jargon. In such cases, consider how your work will be used down the road and how you can help facilitate better communication.

Limit lists of numbers and statistics. Statistics are good and helpful, up to a point, so use them wisely and sparingly. A sit-up-and-take-notice number can take on a life of its own. Too many numbers, like too many words, become noise. The reporter can probably find the unemployment rate, Medicaid enrollment, or life expectancy statistics on their own, so don't feel like you need to provide all the details for the entire story.

You don't know everything. Although you know a lot, you don't know everything. If you are asked something outside your area of expertise, consider responding with "I don't know the answer, but I can tell you that . . ." Of course, how you finish that sentence should be on point and illuminating, not something untethered to the conversation. This might also be an occasion when you can direct the reporter to other people or resources for a more detailed response.

Feel free to hypothesize. Although you may not know everything, you are a researcher, and a core part of your job is to ask questions about the world. Constructing hypotheses is therefore part of your trade. If you have one that bubbles up from your extensive knowledge, consider presenting it, along with attendant clues and the clear statement that you are, in fact, hypothesizing and presenting a conclusion or recommendation that flows from it.

Stay focused. Whether your interview is over the phone, online, face-to-face, or in a studio, stay focused on what is being said and asked. It is surprisingly easy to be distracted or to formulate a response that is out of sync with the conversation.

There is no "no comment." Never use "no comment," which can be taken as "guilty as charged." If you don't have an informed answer, it's perfectly acceptable to say, "I don't know." Better yet is to give the reporter some other resources or people she might contact to get more information.

Repeat the question. Some researchers find it helpful to repeat the question (or a part of it) or to recast it, especially if the original is unclear or unnecessarily negative or testy. For example:

REPORTER: "Why are researchers so slow to answer questions?"

RESEARCHER: "Why do researchers take longer than others to answer questions? Because we are trained to explore the subtleties and ramifications of complex issues, answers must be more thoughtful, deliberate, and grounded in facts. That takes time."

Summarize. It's the rare interview—at least those that are not broadcast live—that doesn't end with the reporter asking, "Is there anything I missed?" or "Anything you want to add?" The answer is always yes. Even if you've covered everything, use this opportunity to repeat or underscore your most important points. Having spoken to the reporter for a few minutes, you may have sputtered through an answer, and this can be your opportunity to make a response more clever or concise. This is also a chance to correct a previous statement or to bring more essential information to the conversation.

The interview is over when the reporter is done. Even when you think the interview is over, it's not. The reporter might be putting away her notepad or the camera crew might be disconnecting their equipment, but a nonchalantly tossed question seeking your opinion about Senator Smith or Proposition 143 could catch you off guard and result in an ill-considered response. The interview is not completely over until you've shaken hands and gone your separate ways. Again, this isn't suggesting that reporters are out to burn you or misrepresent you, but when you're doing an interview, you're always on the record, even after the formalities have concluded.

Radio and Television Interviews

Radio and television have another dimension to consider before agreeing to participate. Especially on television, how you look can often be as important as what you say. On radio, the energy, speed, and tone of your voice can influence listeners' perception of you. Perfection is not required in these interviews (or in interviews generally), but you still want to prepare as best you can.

Radio and TV interviews are often choreographed pro/con conversations. Are you comfortable taking the role of the proponent of one worldview pitted against a contrarian? Try to anticipate opposing points of view—part of your preparation should be to get ready to respond to other perspectives. Your mannerisms can be misinterpreted, so underreact to a surprising or aggressive question or remark—let your carefully chosen words respond, not your voice or face.

There are lots of other things to consider when in front of a camera or microphone, details that are beyond the scope of this chapter. Here is a handful to get started:

- Arrive early at the studio to compose yourself and to acclimate to your surroundings.

- Convey confidence with a strong voice and speak at a moderate, unhurried pace.
- Use short sentences and be succinct. Don't hog the camera or microphone.
- Present as much warmth, interest, and liveliness as you naturally can.
- For TV interviews, wear solid colors, but avoid all white. Leave stripes, plaids, or distracting designs at home, along with large, jangling jewelry.
- Also, look at the reporter or host, not the camera. Maintain good posture. You can lean forward a bit, but don't slouch or squirm. Use your hands for emphasis. Keep nervous habits, such as finger tapping, at bay.

After the Interview

When the interview is really over, immediately follow up with any additional information you promised to send. Alternatively, you may have neglected to mention something essential, or, after replaying your mental tapes, you realize you provided an incorrect or confusing response. Reporters will certainly be grateful that you corrected a mistake or helped clarify a potentially confusing issue.

Connecting after the interview can also help ensure that the reporter has your name, title, and organization correct. And hang on to the reporter's contact information and interests so you can send tips about forthcoming research. Keep an eye on her reporting and send helpful comments to strengthen the source–reporter relationship.

Your presence in the finished story will probably be limited—a quote or two, or a paraphrase, attributed to you. Especially in general-interest media, expect some simplification or condensing. Most readers don't have a doctorate in economics or the capacity to wade through intricate explanations of research methodology. With stories reaching many thousands or even millions of people, your potential to make a powerful, positive impression within your professional circle and the wider public is considerable.

Expert Guidance

Journalist Dan Gorenstein served as senior reporter for the Health Desk at public radio's *Marketplace* show and continues to cover the business of healthcare and the intersection of policy, money, and people. Dan knows his way around a microphone and how to encourage researchers to deliver compact statements that illuminate a bigger story in an ear-friendly way.

At a workshop at the Urban Institute, Dan offered these potent pointers:

> *Context.* Your work often fits within a larger body of research. Put your project into context and explain how your work influences or advances the public's current understanding. An important point to remember is that reporters are like readers diving into the middle of a novel—help them catch up.

> *Big idea.* Boil down your research into the one, two, or, if you must, three most important points for a public audience. It is easy to get lost in details, especially numbers. This can trip up the most intrepid reporters and can even send you down your own rabbit hole. Simplifying what you say—not your content, but the way you say it—can help the reporter better understand your special knowledge and communicate it to her audience.

> *Articulate.* Words matter. Identify the big ideas and then explain them in one or two sentences with as little jargon as possible. Use examples, even if they are hypothetical, and use imagery to convey your content. It's important to practice your answers—pull someone aside and test out your answers to expected questions or how you want to convey your big ideas. A strategy that often works well is to think of an analogy or clever way to talk about your work.

> *Be natural.* The best quotes usually come during a normal conversation, not when someone tries to speak in sound bites. If you are

concerned you are being misunderstood, diplomatically explain that you worry you aren't being clear and explain yourself in a different way. You are the expert in your interactions with reporters, so you can and should feel free to be assertive when necessary.

Control. What you *can* control is making sure you are clear, concise, and cooperative. Practice your answers, consider your primary content, and recognize who the main users are for this media outlet.

Trust yourself. You are the expert. That's an honor and a responsibility.

Preparation Questions: Two Examples

To ready yourself for an interview, role-play the reporter–researcher exchange with a colleague or, if you have one, someone from your media relations staff. Run through the questions you expect to be asked, as well as those troublesome ones you hope won't come your way.

As an example, before releasing a study about the hospital costs of firearm assaults, the research team and I practiced the following questions:

1. Why did you explore this issue?

2. Why haven't others looked at this topic?

3. Why is it important?

4. What findings surprised you or are particularly telling for health-care providers and policymakers?

5. Why are these findings important?

6. What are the implications for the healthcare sector (for example, hospitals, doctors, and nurses) and for policymakers?

7. What recommendations do you have?

8. The victims skew young, male, and poor. Does that have special implications?

9. Your paper implies that uninsured people face diminished care if they are shot. True?

10. Your research is at the intersection of public health and public safety. What should these fields take away from the study? What should they be discussing with each other?

11. What questions remain unanswered for you?

You can use these questions as a framework or starting point for your own practice and preparation. Draft and hone concise, clear answers about your research for an audience who may not have the expertise and knowledge in your field that you do.

As another example, I worked with a researcher who addressed evidence that high-cost tax preparation is disproportionately concentrated in low-income neighborhoods. We practiced a different set of questions:

1. How much of a problem is this?

2. Has there been documentation of fraud, abuse, and gross errors in the tax-preparation industry?

3. Is the industry bad?

4. How much is the tax code to blame?

5. How important is tax season for low-income households?

6. What fees are people being charged for getting their taxes prepared?

7. Why doesn't competition work in this environment?

8. What can be done to improve the situation?

9. Tax Day (April 15) is tomorrow. What can people do who still haven't filed? Where can they go?

Below, I have provided you with a checklist that contains some of the major questions you should be ready for, tips for giving good interviews, and strategies to pull it all together. (A downloadable version is available at the book's website at https://www.urban.org/ ElevatetheDebateBook.)

Wrapping Up

Researchers, scholars, and other experts who interact with members of the media have the opportunity to reach a wider audience for their work, analysis, and ideas. But giving an interview should not be a casual endeavor; it takes concentration and preparation. An interview should also not be viewed as a one-time event. Use it to cultivate a relationship with the media outlet so you can be a resource in the future. Even if you are not interviewed this time, or if you are interviewed but not quoted in the final story, there's always a next time, a next story, another issue.

If your job doesn't involve interacting with the media, you still likely present your work to colleagues and managers, maybe even thought leaders and decisionmakers. Many of the strategies discussed earlier are just as applicable to those situations: prepare your work and your answers, speak clearly and slowly, possibly repeat the question, limit lists and jargon when not needed, and find the big idea you want people to grab on to.

The tools and techniques laid out in this chapter will enable you to give interviews that provide information and insights deftly to reporters, who in turn can communicate them to their audiences. Your responsibility is to recognize that *you* are the expert and that the reporter is coming to you for your expertise. Reporters are not there to try to burn you or misquote you. They are there doing their jobs to help explain an issue to their readers, listeners, or viewers.

As you prepare for your interview or meeting, identify the central ideas you want to convey. Practice honing your responses for those who may not be experts in your field and who want to learn more. Working with the media is your opportunity to share insights and help readers and others experience those same discoveries and maybe bring about positive change. When you finally do give that interview, be relaxed, confident, and in control. And have fun.

Key Takeaways

- Reporters are seeking you out because you are an expert. They are trying to learn from you so they can better educate their readers, listeners, or viewers.

- Make sure you are willing and available to conduct the interview. You may need to prepare yourself or reread some of your work. Reporters are looking to you for your expertise, so make your time and their time useful.

- Practice your responses out loud, preferably with someone who can provide helpful feedback.

- Most interviews end with a catchall question such as, "Do you have anything to add?" The answer to this question is always yes—take the opportunity to correct any mistakes you may have made during the interview, or make a previous answer more concise or punchier.

Your Checklist to Success

Key takeaways

- ❏ What are the two or three most interesting or important findings from your research?
- ❏ Why are they significant?
- ❏ What surprised you?
- ❏ Are there a few statistics that are particularly noteworthy?
- ❏ What are the policy implications of your research and findings?

Interview tips

- ❏ Be confident
- ❏ Take your time

- ❑ Speak in lay terms
- ❑ Be concise
- ❑ Listen carefully
- ❑ Don't be afraid to ask for clarification
- ❑ Don't feel obligated to answer every question or every part of a question

Getting quoted

- ❑ Tell a story
- ❑ Use imagery
- ❑ Spotlight a standout number
- ❑ Bust myths and misperceptions

Problem questions

- ❑ "While I'm not an expert on that subject, I can tell you . . ."
- ❑ "It's too early to tell, but it seems clear . . ."
- ❑ "What's important to remember is . . ."

Keeping it crisp and concise

- ❑ "The bottom line is that . . ."
- ❑ "The three most important reasons . . ."
- ❑ "To summarize . . ."

Putting it together

- ❑ Be quick and responsive, even if it's a referral to another source, when a media request arrives
- ❑ Think through your key takeaways
- ❑ Make the information accessible
- ❑ You're the expert: you can drive the conversation
- ❑ Say something that stands out
- ❑ Practice, practice, practice

Case Study: *Quick responses to policy proposals pay off for elite media cultivation*

The Urban Institute's Safety Net to Solid Ground Initiative illustrates how organizations can work with the media to share their insights with policymakers and educate the public. The initiative was designed to respond to policy proposals and debates shaping safety net programs (such as the Supplemental Nutrition Assistance Program, or SNAP) with evidence-based insights. The initiative has become a trusted source for elite national media, as well as local and regional press, seeking to understand the effects of major policy changes that are remaking the social safety net.

In one of its first analyses, researchers scrutinized a proposal that allows states to introduce work requirements into Medicaid as a condition of eligibility. In a media landscape that now requires quicker turnaround than ever before, researchers dropped everything to examine how a legislative proposal in Kentucky and Arkansas could affect enrollees' coverage. Their quick responses to reporters' queries landed them coverage in local and national media, including the *New York Times*, the *Los Angeles Times*, and outlets in Kentucky and Arkansas.

When the U.S. House Agriculture Committee proposed a farm bill that would have intensified work requirements in the SNAP program, the research team forecast the number of people who would likely lose their benefits as a result. The researchers made time for media interviews before and after the Agriculture Committee vote, even when competing project deadlines made it inconvenient. As a result, they received coverage in national outlets such as NPR, CBS News, and CityLab. The researchers worked with Urban's media team to test answers to questions, gather additional background information and data, and fine-tune their takeaway messages. Although all of this required more of their time, the additional preparation led to better interviews and more media coverage.

The *Safety Net* initiative also earned media coverage on its findings from Urban's annual survey of household material hardship and well-being. The first report published from this survey featured a reporter-friendly "sit up and take notice" statistic: that nearly 40 percent of American adults struggle to meet their basic needs for food, housing, and medical care. The Associated Press published this shocking finding, which led to a cascade of stories and editorials in major newspapers across the country, as well as significant television, radio, and online coverage.

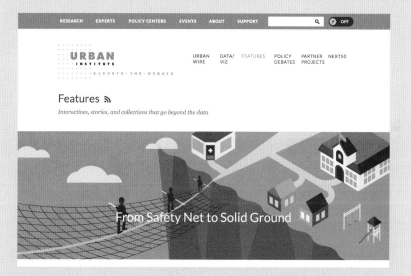

The Safety Net to Solid Ground Initiative's quick response to policy proposals shows how taking the time to respond to topics in the news cycle can pay rich dividends for elite media cultivation.

chapter seven

Social Media Can Build Audiences That Matter

David Connell

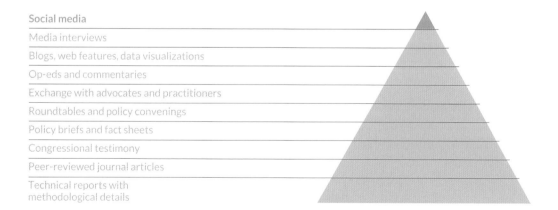

Social media

Media interviews

Blogs, web features, data visualizations

Op-eds and commentaries

Exchange with advocates and practitioners

Roundtables and policy convenings

Policy briefs and fact sheets

Congressional testimony

Peer-reviewed journal articles

Technical reports with methodological details

Social media platforms like Twitter, Facebook, and LinkedIn give you the opportunity to connect and converse with new and influential audiences around your work in ways that are both intimate and public. These platforms can help you connect with anyone: colleagues around the world, decisionmakers in your and other organizations, policymakers, and, perhaps more important, members of their staff. And they allow you to make these connections in ways that facilitate one-on-one conversations, but let the world see that you are connecting—and potentially influencing—important stakeholders and thought leaders.

There are real barriers and dangers to engaging in social media, however, and it can seem difficult to break through the noise. Engaging in social media conversations can seem intimidating and fruitless, particularly when you are starting out. This chapter is designed to help you engage on social media platforms in ways that feel comfortable and productive and do not distract from your existing work. In short, I want social media to help you advance your work, not distract you from it.

Some goals to think about when engaging in social media:

- Find an audience of colleagues, thought leaders, and changemakers who are interested in your work and can act on it.
- Provide content that includes blog posts, research papers, the work of colleagues and other professionals, and third-party trusted news sources related to your area of expertise.
- Have a strategy that allows you to focus on one or two social media platforms and doesn't become a burden.
- Become a trusted source of information in your field who engages on social media in a kind and productive way, perhaps even with a touch of humor.

If your experience engaging in social media consists of posting photos of your kids or vacations to Facebook, using social media to achieve professional goals and content sharing may seem daunting. Despite the increased prevalence of social media in the policy world—and our culture at large—many analysts and experts remain unconvinced that engaging in social media is a productive use of their time. My goal is to convince you it is. First, I show how policymakers and influencers use social media and how it can impact how people find out about your work. Then I explain how to use three major social media platforms—Twitter, LinkedIn, and Facebook—to help you better communicate your work and advance your professional goals.

Making the Case for Social Media

There are two primary reasons for researchers to engage in social media. First, social media has become a driver of conversations around the world. Policymakers, especially in Washington, DC, use social media to help inform their decisions. Second, social media platforms inform online search results and ultimately make you more visible when colleagues, journalists, and policymakers search for you online.

Do People Really Use This Stuff?

This is one of the most common questions skeptical content producers ask about using social media to inform and influence policymakers and decisionmakers. They don't see how a tweet or LinkedIn post could possibly reach someone with the power to shape policy.

Survey data tell us that social media is especially important for policymakers. Since 2002, the *National Journal* has surveyed a broad swath of "Washington insiders" that include Capitol Hill staffers, federal executives, lobbyists, researchers, analysts, and journalists. The survey provides a complete and in-depth picture of how these decisionmakers consume media and what is influencing them.

The 2017 survey (conducted between May and June of that year) showed that social media has high scores as a resource used to influence others when "preparing for a critical vote." Other sources that scored high on this scale included research reports, news publications and websites, and infographics and charts. All of these can be leveraged and spread through social media. This most recent *National Journal* survey also found that social media usage among insiders is prevalent and well established for both personal and professional purposes. Among those surveyed, 85 percent report using Facebook in the last six months, 79 percent report using LinkedIn, and 65 percent report using Twitter.

And they are not just using social media on their lunch breaks. Many see social media platforms as part of the work that they do, with 51 percent saying social media is "an important part of my daily work" and 29 percent saying they rely on social media to "help formulate my opinions." These numbers are even higher among Capitol Hill staffers: 69 percent said social media is an important part of their daily work, and 31 percent said that what they find on social media helps formulate their opinions.

It is clear that social media has become an integral part of the conversation among Washington insiders and policymakers, particularly those on Capitol Hill. They are engaging on social media to gather information, inform decisions, and persuade others to back those decisions. If you want your research to influence these decisions—or even reach state and local policymakers, journalists, or other influencers and researchers—participating in the social media conversation is increasingly a must.

But Isn't This All Just Fake News?

Reports have revealed how fraudulent websites and social media accounts may have influenced the 2016 U.S. presidential election and continue to spread false and misleading information. The problem has become so prevalent that social media platforms have struggled to monitor the information spread on their networks and prevent the spread of false and misleading information. This is a defining crisis for social media companies and one they will need to address if they are going to remain useful and productive tools.

Survey results from the 2017 *National Journal* report already showed the effects of the fake-news phenomenon. In many areas, trust and use of social media had ticked downward slightly compared with 2016. Some social media companies are already taking steps to delete false and misleading content from their platforms. State and federal policymakers are also considering actions to potentially regulate the industry. With billions of users and dollars at stake, private companies and government will likely take action to address these issues and try to restore trust in how people share and use information.

You Are Who Google Says You Are

In addition to influencing ongoing conversations, social media platforms are a great way to help people find you on the Internet. Not only do you become instantly searchable on these social media platforms, but your social media presence feeds into, and helps boost, your presence on the world's most important homepage: Google.

Having a high-ranking and a robust presence on Google search results for your name can be an asset to your professional growth and ability to have influence. When a stakeholder, funder, or Hill Staffer searches for you on Google and finds you in one of the top results, multiple pages mentioning your name, and photos of you speaking at a conference, they are far more likely to view you as a trusted source.

The same goes for other researchers or academics. If you are presenting at a conference, and a colleague wants to better understand your expertise or read your work, a well-rounded search engine result can provide instant credibility.

Social media profiles—particularly Twitter and LinkedIn—are indexed by the Google search engine and can have an important influence over time on how you appear in search results. This is because social media platforms are indexed by Google *and* are trusted sources of information. The algorithms Google uses to generate ranks in your search results are not published, but we do know that the following factors have a positive influence on Google rankings:

- A well-maintained and up-to-date university or organization bio page with a photo
- A well-maintained and up-to-date publications page

- A consistent blogging presence
- An up-to-date LinkedIn account
- Participation on other social media platforms
- A consistent name and affiliation across all these pages and services
- Linking as many of these profiles together (for instance, your bio page, Twitter profile, and LinkedIn page should all be connected)

Google likes consistent, well-maintained, and frequently updated content that links together. Social media accounts, particularly Twitter and LinkedIn, meet all these criteria.

Twitter, LinkedIn, and Facebook: An Overview of Major Platforms

There are dozens of social media platforms with billions of users (see the *Other Social Media Platforms* box), but only a few are right for finding and engaging with your colleagues and policymakers—particularly Twitter, LinkedIn, and Facebook. These three largest social media platforms are, according to the *National Journal*'s annual reports, those most commonly used by policymakers and other influencers.

Although a presence on all of these platforms might seem beneficial, you likely need to maintain a robust presence on only one or two. The platform you choose to be the most active on will, simply put, be the one that most appeals to you, based on a range of criteria including your target audience, the functionality of the site (and mobile app), and the type of content that performs well on the platform.

Other Social Media Platforms
Not all social media platforms are appropriate for sharing your findings. But as technology evolves and people's interactions with these platforms change, it is worth noting that there are dozens of other services that may change or become more popular in the years to come.

YouTube is a video-sharing platform on which users watch a billion hours of videos every day. YouTube might be valuable if you want to share videos of you speaking or participating in an event. You can also set up a channel to host a collection of videos, such as specific tutorials or teaching videos.

Reddit, which bills itself as "the front page of the Internet," is a discussion website where people can start or join forums called subreddits to share news and content. Reddit casts a wide net across the Internet and it's very likely you'll find a "subreddit" related to your work. This may not be the place to start your social media journey, but it can be a fruitful place once you become well-versed in social media.

Image-sharing platforms like Instagram and Pinterest hold promise for sharing *visual* research and content. On Instagram, for example, users post images, photos, and videos, which you could use to show data visualizations, presentation slides, or images from your speaking events. More recently, users have been writing "long-form captions" on Instagram to share stories and insights related to their images.

Messaging tools like Messenger (which used to be a tool within Facebook) and Snapchat are probably not the place you would currently share your work, but these tools may be used differently in the future. Also, because of cultural factors, government regulations, and differences in technology, some platforms are very popular in certain countries but not in others. For example, WeChat and QQ are extremely popular in China, Line is popular in Japan, and Viber is popular in Eastern Europe.

Jumping into the Twitter Stream

Twitter is one of the more confusing and misunderstood social media platforms. With its esoteric nomenclature (tweets, threads, replies,

@username, hashtags) and its old rule of 140 characters or fewer, Twitter had a pretty high barrier of entry for people unfamiliar with how it works. It is, however, as the *National Journal* survey showed, one of the most popular platforms among the policy-making audience.

What is Twitter exactly? In essence, Twitter is a real-time network where users post updates (tweets) to a timeline visible to anyone visiting their profile page. Other users can comment on those tweets or repost ("retweet") them (with or without comment) to their own timeline. Tweets can be only text or can include links to web pages, photos, images, or videos. Tweets are currently capped at 280 characters, and users can "thread" tweets together to share multiple pieces of content or longer thoughts on a topic.

This tweet from the Urban Institute in August 2018 includes a short description and link to an Urban blog post: https://twitter.com/urbaninstitute/status/1032698235444518912

The default privacy option on a user's Twitter account is open, so anyone visiting a user's Twitter profile page can see all of their tweets.

In addition, tweets are often embedded in news stories and blog posts to provide context or color to a story. Twitter users can make their accounts private and control who has access to view their tweets. Under this scenario, users have to request permission to view tweets, which severely limits the reach of a Twitter account.

What is Twitter good for? A common refrain from those who haven't used Twitter is, "Why do people want to know what I ate for lunch?" I am not sure where that impression came from exactly, but I can assure you the primary use-case for Twitter is sharing information to a group of people with similar interests and having conversations about that information.

Common uses of Twitter include the following:

- Connecting with reporters, peers, and other influencers
- Keeping up with news and information from your field
- Positioning yourself as a curator of interesting, relevant content and analysis pertaining to your area of expertise
- Promoting your own work as it relates to your field
- Promoting the work of trusted colleagues as it relates to your field
- Boosting your profile on Google and other search engines

A typical Twitter interaction for a researcher is to post a tweet linking to a paper or blog post, mentioning a reporter or colleague in the tweet, and then starting a conversation about that paper or blog post. In the best cases, this conversation will result in the reporter using the research in a news story or a colleague citing it in their work. Ideally, the researcher would then tweet a link to the resulting news story or the colleague's work creating a circle of promotion and conversation. Because Twitter is an open social network, other users would be able to see, retweet, and comment on these tweets.

How do you get started on Twitter? Like all social networks, the first thing to do is start an account that includes your name, a bio, and profile picture. Twitter also allows you to include a link in your Twitter profile. A link to your organization bio, your blog, or a publications listing is a good candidate for this space (remember what Google is looking for).

Twitter also requires you to select a username, which is what appears in your tweets and which people use to mention you—it's what appears after the "@" symbol. You may be tempted to put in something whimsical or personal in this space—maybe "@ChubbyHubby42." If you are using Twitter for professional purposes, however, avoid this. No one wants to carry on a conversation about the racial wealth gap with @ChubbyHubby42. The best thing to use as your handle is your full name (e.g., @davidconnell) or some variation of your full name (e.g., @dconnell). If you don't want to use your name, then something related to your work will suffice, such as @socialmediadave.

Here is an example of a profile set up well for Twitter:

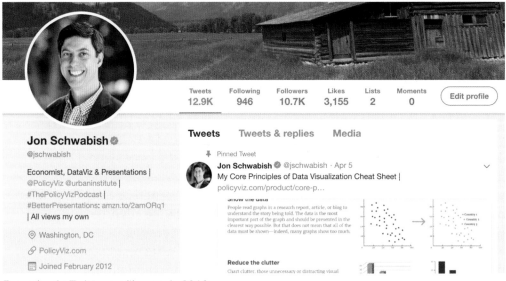

Example of a Twitter profile page in 2019

It has a recognizable photo, a clear bio, and link to an external site. Jon has also "pinned" an important tweet to the top of the page so his new followers can see what he's all about. Pinning tweets allows you to place an important tweet at the top of your profile page that will not change even as you continue to publish more content.

In contrast, this profile does not include a photo, bio, or a full name. This account is obviously not set up for professional purposes.

Example of a Twitter profile page in 2019.

Once you have your profile set up, the next step is to start sharing content. You can share links to what you're reading, your own blog posts and research papers, news stories related to your field, or the work of colleagues and collaborators. Anything you find interesting and think others like you might find interesting is fodder for sharing. When you tweet, try to mention the username of the person (if they are on Twitter) who wrote the piece you are sharing. Sharing other users' tweets (retweeting) is another way to generate content and information for your network; you can simply retweet an existing tweet, or you can add a comment to your retweet, maybe to give your (short) perspective, endorsement, or critique.

Tweets with images are usually more engaging than tweets with just text. Most news articles and websites now use "Twitter cards" that will automatically generate a visual element in the tweet instead of a simple text link; the previous Urban Institute tweet, for example, was written with a simple URL, but Twitter automatically converted it to a picture when it was posted. Sharing graphs, charts, .GIFs (a series of images stitched together that moves as an animation), short videos, and other interesting visual content always makes for great tweets.

Every time you mention a username on Twitter, retweet something, comment on a tweet, or participate in a conversation, you are letting people know you are active on Twitter. If they are interested in what you're sharing, they will follow you, and your social network will grow. In essence, the more active you are on Twitter, the more followers you will gain, and the more your influence you will grow.

That being said, some people are still reluctant to contribute content to Twitter. This is totally understandable; if not used well and carefully, social media can result in embarrassment, harassment fights, addiction, and more. One way to get a feel for Twitter is to use it as a real-time library or news feed. You can simply follow publications and people you want to receive content from and view that content. This will allow you to get a feel for the service without having to generate original content.

Once you're ready to share content, you can start posting your own work and thoughts, or sharing what other people have posted. Before you start actively following other people, make sure you have at least 20 to 30 tweets. You want to have a good body of work built up so potential followers can see that you are active and have interesting things to say. Once you have that stock of tweets under your belt, you can start following others, which is the best way to build your network.

As an example of how *not* to start out on Twitter, several years ago I received an email newsletter from a professional organization that its new CEO was joining Twitter to better engage with colleagues, constituents, and the public. The newsletter promised engaging and thought-provoking tweets from the new CEO, but when I clicked on the link to his Twitter page, I found a nice profile page with zero tweets. I did not follow the new CEO and still don't know if he ever had anything interesting to say.

The best way to find people to follow is to survey your current professional network to find out if they use Twitter and follow those who do (they will receive a notification that you're following them and can then follow you back). This will create an initial network that is likely to support you and help you grow on the platform. You should also follow people who are in your field and whose work you are familiar with, though you may not know personally. Another way to find people to follow is Twitter's "Who to Follow" recommendation engine, which tracks who you follow, what you tweet about, and who you mention in tweets, and then suggests like-minded accounts to follow.

Try to maintain a reasonable ratio of people who follow you to the number of people you follow. You don't want to follow 5,000 people if only 5 people are following you—it makes it look like people aren't interested in what you have to say. The same holds true for how many people are following you. Don't worry about the number of followers you have; it is far better to have 120 great followers who are in your professional network, interested in your work, and who have influence than it is to have 1,200 followers who are only interested in fighting or gossiping about issues you don't care about.

Taking it to the next level. After you have your Twitter account set up, you're familiar with posting tweets, you're following some people, and you have your core followers, it's time to bring it to the next level. Here are some things to try:

- **Show a little personality.** Although your main objective is to promote and share your work and influence policy, people aren't all work and no play. It's fine to talk about some of your personal interests and hobbies. This will help people connect with you on a more personal level.

- **Download the Twitter mobile app.** Twitter is a great way to scan the news and find interesting things to read and react to during downtime. Having the app on your phone helps you be more active on Twitter.

- **Tweet early and tweet often.** A good goal is to tweet at least two to three times a day. This can be difficult when you are working. To help facilitate more regular tweeting, you can use a third-party service that will store tweets for you and release them through-out the day. This way, you can create tweets during your morning reading time that will be published automatically throughout the day. Buffer, Hootsuite, and TweetDeck from Twitter all offer free tools that allow users to schedule tweets for later posting.

- **Experiment.** Although the character count inherent in Twitter may feel like a hindrance, there are many ways to experiment and be creative. Replies, images, the ability to easily include .GIFs and vid-eos, and the ability to thread tweets provide users with the ability to express themselves more freely. Threaded tweets, or a series of tweets strung together, give users a lot of flexibility to be creative on Twitter. This tweet from Stephanie Hicks, an assistant professor in the Department of Biostatistics at Johns Hopkins University, for example, is just the first in a series of tweets she posted in March 2019 about her co-authored paper that had just been released.

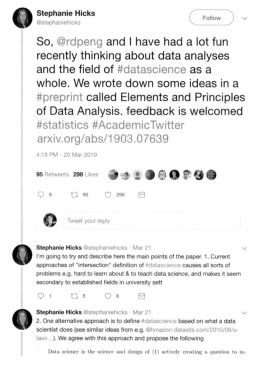

Source: Reproduced by permission of Stephanie Hicks, https://twitter.com/stephaniehicks/status/1108462768099856384.

Making effective connections. A common misconception about Twitter is that it functions primarily, or even exclusively, as a passive source of information: Users tweet links or content, other users consume that content, like it, or retweet it, without much further interaction. Although this is certainly one use case, it is not *the best* use-case for the platform.

Twitter users are most effective when they are engaging with other users, commenting on their content and sharing content with them directly. For those hoping to influence policy with their research, engaging the right users directly on Twitter in a public way, can be very effective.

Here are some examples based on real-life scenarios:

- *Engaging with influencers*. Beth is an influential thinker in the nonprofit world. She publishes a popular blog on running small nonprofits, is a frequent speaker at nonprofit conferences, and consults for nonprofit readers. Mary, a nonprofit researcher, uses some of Beth's work in a new report on managing Head Start programs. When the report is published, Mary tweets at Beth (using Beth's Twitter handle so she receives a notification) telling her about the work. The two discuss the paper on Twitter, and Beth writes a blog post about the new work, exposing Mary's report to a large target audience of small nonprofit professionals.

- *Engaging with journalists*. Dara is an immigration-policy reporter for a daily news site covering social policy with a large and influential audience. Maria, an immigration researcher, has a new paper with insights on the progress of third-generation Latino immigrants. When her paper is published, Maria tweets out a link to the paper with her topline findings. Dara reads the paper, downloads some of its compelling charts, and has a conversation with Maria over Twitter's direct message system (a private messaging system) to collect quotes from her. She writes an article that broadcasts Maria's work to thousands of more readers than it would have reached otherwise.

LinkedIn: A Professional Place to Develop Content

LinkedIn has been around long enough for me to assume that you are familiar with its basic premise: You can create a profile, an online résumé, connect with colleagues, and receive updates when they receive a new job. This basic functionality is valuable when looking for a new job but doesn't compel you to come back and interact with colleagues.

Several years ago, LinkedIn started adding new features that allows users to create, join, and interact in professional groups, which allowed for further networking. More recently, LinkedIn has introduced features that allow users to post content from other websites and blogs to their LinkedIn page. They have also created an editor that allows users to create simple blog posts within the LinkedIn platform.

These changes have made LinkedIn a more interactive platform where users can create and share content and ideas with their networks of professional colleagues. These features, combined with the increasingly personal nature of Facebook, means that LinkedIn is now widely seen as the place to connect with colleagues and like-minded professionals. At the Urban Institute, starting in 2016, we started to see a marked increase in website traffic coming from LinkedIn. Similarly, some of our researchers now see the majority of their site traffic coming from LinkedIn.

LinkedIn's feed page (https://www.linkedin.com/feed/) is your de-facto homepage and functions similarly to the Facebook news-feed. It includes your profile photo, articles, and links created by those in your network, and trending stories (of course, how these are organized have changed at various points and are sure to change again). There is also space to either share a piece of content or write a blog post ("write an article"). This is a great place to share links to your research or, if you don't have a blog, to begin to establish a blogging presence (see Chapter 5 for other blogging platforms).

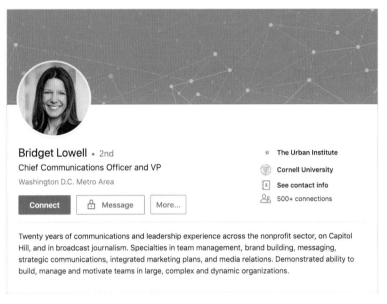

Example of a LinkedIn profile page in 2019.

The guidelines for posting content and interacting with users on LinkedIn are similar to those of Twitter, except you want to concentrate on posting content that you've created. On Twitter, depending on the amount of original content, you may find that much of your feed should be links to other people's content related to your field. If you have enough original content, you probably want to strive for a 50-50 split between your content and sharing other people's content. Remember, Twitter is sometimes about volume, so you are going to need to curate other people's content as well. Both strategies will help establish you as a *curator* of relevant content. On LinkedIn, it's all about sharing *your* unique expertise and insight, so you want to concentrate on content you have written, creating blog posts, or sharing news articles where you or your work are cited.

When thinking about your presence on LinkedIn (or any social media platform) follow these guidelines to maintain your voice and your identity:

- Be a source of ideas, good original concepts, humor, and expertise in your field.

- Hone your insights, your ideas, your narrative, and the things you're known for.
- Be thoughtful about who you follow, how you position yourself, and participate in the dialogue.

Making Connections on LinkedIn

Like many social media tools, how people connect on LinkedIn has evolved along with the platform. In the early "online résumé days," most users held only strong-tie connections—they only connected with people with whom they had a professional or, perhaps, personal relationship. There's a standard joke that you know someone is looking for a new job when you're notified they've updated their LinkedIn page.

As LinkedIn has evolved to include more ways to post content and interact, how people engage with each other has also changed. It is now common to follow someone on LinkedIn with whom you *do not* have strong ties, but with whom you share common professional interests. Following someone will allow his content to show up in your feed so you can learn about what he's posting. Similarly, someone who you don't know, but who shares your professional interests, may follow you on LinkedIn so he can see your content in his feed. This "follower" dynamic is similar to that of Twitter.

It's possible that you have a LinkedIn page that you do not update regularly or to which you post content, but one that has garnered several hundred strong-tie connections. If this is the case, it is worth revisiting your LinkedIn page, updating your profile, and beginning to share content with your existing connections. As you do, you will likely find that other professionals in your space will find your content and begin following you and sharing with you.

Sharing Content on LinkedIn

LinkedIn allows users to share links, images, videos, and write blog posts through the feed page. It also allows you to "tag" LinkedIn users in posts so they will be notified of your posts (you can also allow or disallow comments). Unlike the basic operation of Twitter, there are different privacy settings for LinkedIn content that can be selected whenever you post something new to the platform.

The type of content you should share on LinkedIn is similar to the bulk of what you would share on Twitter: professionally focused content that will interest and educate other researchers, policymakers, journalists, and influencers. One major difference I recommend for LinkedIn is that you keep the content you share confined to what directly references you or your work. At its heart, LinkedIn is still a professional résumé builder, so you want to post content that is going to directly show your expertise and work. For example:

- Links to research you've published online in journals or other websites (be sure to tag any co-authors currently on LinkedIn)
- Links to blog posts or articles you've written—again, tag any co-authors or editors
- Links to news articles that quote you or cite your work
- Links to conferences, events, seminars, or webinars where you will be presenting
- Videos that feature you or your work
- A blog post you've written based on your work, observations, a new policy proposal, or even notes from a conference you've recently attended

Sharing this type of rich and varied content from your career will help build your profile on LinkedIn, increase its value when you show up in search engine results, and help you connect with other LinkedIn users who share your professional expertise.

Facebook: Creating Groups

The final social media platform is the largest of the three, with more than 2 billion registered users. Connections on Facebook are "strong-tie" connections—friends and family members—while Twitter and LinkedIn are "weak-tie" networks more likely to consist of professional associations and people you might not even know. Thus, I don't recommend Facebook for professional connections because Facebook networks tend to be made up of strong-tie connections from a wide variety of social groups—family members, current friends, former high school and college friends, coworkers (current and former), and everything in between. These social groups primarily share personal content in the form of family photos, politically focused news stories, political memes, sports stories, information on their hobbies, and (again) everything in between.

I do, however, think that Facebook groups (https://www.facebook.com/groups/) are one way to use Facebook to develop a professional community of researchers, academics, and thought leaders. Facebook groups operate in the same way as the ubiquitous Facebook homepage, allowing users to post content and carry on discussions around that content on a continuous feed. The primary difference is that Facebook groups allow you to invite select people and separate group content from your high school friends and aunts and uncles. In a Facebook group, you can invite your colleagues to share and discuss their work without the distraction of pictures from your friend's latest camping trip (my recommendation is to create a closed group, which requires the group administrator to approve applications to the group). Facebook groups are a terrific way to create stronger ties with colleagues you know now or want to get to know. Who knows, you may even develop a new research partner.

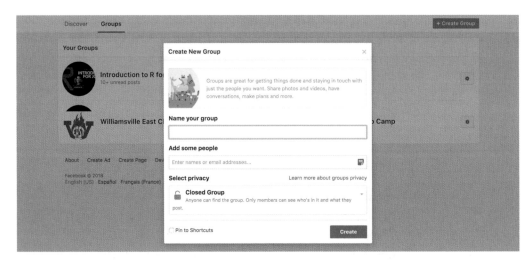

Screenshot of creating a Facebook Group in 2019

Who You Should Invite to Your Group and What Should You Post

Invite professional colleagues you know or want to get to know to your group. These should be people who you would want to have coffee with at a conference to discuss work in your field because, at its core, this is what you will be doing in your group. Start small and allow the group to grow through connections. If you invite 10 colleagues and the discussion is lively and informative, each of those colleagues will likely want to invite other members. As the group administrator, you will always have control over who is allowed into the group.

What Kind of Content Should You Post to Your Group?

The content you post to the group is anything that would be of professional interest to your colleagues. Again, the idea behind groups is for people to converse with each other around the content, so when you post content, also pose questions and try to elicit conversation. Managing a thriving Facebook group can take time, but it can also be rewarding. You should try to provoke as much conversation as possible and engage as many members as you can. As the group grows and engages, this work will be shared across the group, with all members sharing content and sparking conversations.

Social Media and Your Health and Safety

While social media can be a great tool for connecting with colleagues and getting your work into the hands of decisionmakers and thought leaders, it can also create distractions when you need to get work done. In extreme cases, social media can harm your mental health and open you up to threats and harassment.

Social Media Sites Are Designed to Be Addictive

It is now clear that social media use can be habit-forming and some research suggests that users can develop social media addictions akin to substance abuse and behavioral addictive disorders. It is also now well-documented that social media companies use design techniques and user experience techniques that keep users returning to their sites and applications and, once there, keep them on the platform for as long as possible. According to researchers from the Digital Addiction team at Bournemouth University in England, these techniques include:

- **Scarcity:** This occurs when a social media post is only available for a short time (such as on Snapchat) or quickly scrolls by the user "in real time" as posts do on Twitter. Scarcity keeps users coming back to a site or scrolling through a site, so they don't miss what's been shown.
- **Social proof:** The use of likes, retweets, and follower/friend counts on social media platforms provide users with a (sometimes empty) sense of popularity and validation. This can cause users to "chase numbers" with sensational clickbait content rather than content that has true value. It can also make you want to stay on the platform longer, looking for validation.
- **Personalization:** As you share and like more content on a social media platform, the tools' algorithms learn more about you and increasingly serve you more personalized content or follower suggestions. This content, tailored just for you, keeps you on the platform longer.
- **Reciprocity:** As you invite and accumulate more friends, the platforms signal your popularity on the network with a score, which encourages you to continue using them. The accumulation of friends on a platform also makes it more difficult to leave.

Managing Social Media Usage

If you find that you are spending too much time on social media, there are several strategies you can use to help manage your time more wisely.

- **Remove social media apps from your phone**. Just like social media apps, our smartphones are designed to be habit-forming and keep you coming back. If you find you're spending too much time on your phone, delete your social media and apps from it. You can still post interesting articles to social media through an app like

Buffer, but you will no longer be compelled to check, swipe, or scroll through social media. In his book *Digital Minimalism*, author Cal Newton recommends "intentionally and aggressively cleaning away low-value digital noise, and optimizing your use of the tools that really matter."

- **Use a monitoring app like Apple's Screen Time.** These apps monitor how much time you spend on your phone. You'll likely be shocked by how much time you spend on your phone. Once you know the numbers and what's occupying your time, you can work on putting yourself on a social media diet.

- **Use site blockers to keep you focused.** When you're on a desktop or laptop at work, a quick click can take you over to a social media site and away from work for potentially hours. To help stay focused, you can use a series of site blocking browser extensions like StayFocusd, WasteNoTime, and RescueTime that will literally prevent you from visiting specific websites.

- **Treat social media as a task.** A smart way to manage social media without using external tools is to simply treat social media as a work task. That is, set aside a set time during the workday to update and browse your social media accounts—right before, during, or after lunch is a good time. You can also use a "social media break" as a reward for completing a set task.

Social Media Harassment

Unfortunately, using social media can also mean opening yourself up to harassment. This is particularly true if you are engaging in conversations on politically sensitive or controversial topics. Social media allows people with overly strong political views to issue threats, or harass opponents from the safety of the screen, often without retaliation. Women and minority groups are more likely to be targeted.

If you are being harassed on a social media platform, there are several steps you should take immediately:

- **Don't respond.** In general, responding to online harassment only leads to an escalation of that harassment. Sometimes, responding will even spur others to join the harassment.

- **Report the abuse to the platform**. Social media tools have guidelines regarding harassment and reporting the harassment can get the user taken off the platform. Reporting harassment is often as easy as reporting the offending social media post.
- **Blocking the user.** If a particular user is harassing you repeatedly, you should continue to report the abuse to the company and also block the user from seeing your social media profile or engaging with your account. The user will not know he or she has been blocked, but you they will no longer be able to see your content or profile on the platform.
- **Take broader action**. If you are being harassed online through multiple social media platforms or channels, you should document that abuse and report it to your online service provider and, in some cases, law enforcement. There are resources at the US government website https://www.stopbullying.gov/ for reporting online harassment.
- **Find support.** Online harassment can take an emotional toll on you and cause undue stress. If you find you need support after an incident of online harassment, there are places to find it, such as HeartMob, an online community where people facing harassment and abuse can come together and offer support. HeartMob also includes tools that allow you to report online abuse across multiple platforms.

Tying It All Together to Amplify Your Voice

Using these social media strategies will enable you to amplify your voice, reach other colleagues you might not reach in the "real world," and connect directly with reporters, policymakers, and others who can use your research to inform their work. This won't magically happen, however, just by setting up a Twitter, LinkedIn, and Facebook accounts—you must deploy these tools in strategic ways to help amplify your voice.

As the pyramid diagram shows, successful social media outreach campaigns start with a solid piece of underlying research. Moving up the pyramid, you (and a media team, should you have access to one) can then leverage communications tools and platforms to get that analysis into the hands of the people who can use it.

To make your way to the top of the pyramid where social media becomes part of your communication strategy, roughly four steps are important. First, conduct in-depth research that is relevant to a major issue, the current news cycle, or has a surprising conclusion. Second, use that research to create an easy-to-understand, visually interesting communications project. This project can range from a narrative feature that explores the research through human stories, to a blog post, or to an interactive data visualization. Third, work on traditional media outreach using *both* the report and the communications product to help show reporters how it can be done (also see Chapter 6). Finally, reinforce that media outreach with a robust social media strategy that promotes the in-depth work, communications product, any news articles that result from the media outreach, and any social media mentions from influential researchers, decisionmakers, or journalists.

Wrapping Up

For people who want to reach a broader audience with their work, inform thought leaders, and affect policy decisions on the local, state, or federal level, simply publishing research and relying on a press release is no longer enough to cut through the overcrowded media landscape. The good news is, social media platforms like Twitter, LinkedIn, and Facebook provide ways to reach and directly engage with others in your profession and those you want to influence. Instead of hoping a colleague, journalist, policymaker, or changemaker finds and reads your work, you now have the power to reach out to them directly and publicly with that work.

Creating and managing a social media presence definitely adds another layer of work, but once the groundwork is laid, the rewards of engaging in social media can be significant. It can increase the value and impact of your work, connect you with colleagues you otherwise would not be able to meet, and provide you with a fun and creative outlet for your thoughts and views.

Key Takeaways

- Social media allows you to connect and engage directly with colleagues, journalists, and lawmakers who may become interested in your work.
- Make sure you have a strategy and a plan for how you are going to use social media and other tools to promote your work to target audiences.
- Social-media success will not come overnight. With consistency, you can develop a robust and influential presence.
- It is not necessary to be professionally active across all social media platforms. Experiment, find one you enjoy working with, and build your presence around it.

Case Study: *Leveraging Twitter to benefit your research*

Matt Chingos, director of Urban's Center on Education Data and Policy, takes time out of almost every day to tweet. It may be a link to his own research, the work of a scholar outside Urban, or photos of his commute to work.

Chingos's (@chingos) Twitter following of more than 6,000 accounts may not be high by celebrity standards, but in the research world, he's built a robust community of academics, graduate students, and media professionals interested in education policy. Although he maintains a professional persona, he's not afraid to make a joke or talk in a more casual tone on the platform.

Chingos didn't have a clear strategy with his Twitter account when he created his profile nearly a decade ago. But he found the more he tweeted and followed people in the education policy space, the more engagement he saw. "It takes patience, and you have to consistently use it. But you can get something out of Twitter," Chingos says. "You can build a community of people who will engage with you."

One key factor in seeing more engagement: He doesn't exclusively tweet his own work. He highlights publications from other organizations and offers his take on new studies and developments in education policy.

Beyond securing a higher profile within the education research space, Chingos has also leveraged his strong Twitter presence to benefit his work. Throughout 2018 and 2019, Urban's Center on Education Data and Policy rolled out their Education Data Portal, an online tool designed to make education data more accessible to reporters, stakeholders, and other researchers. When Urban updates the portal, Chingos lets his Twitter followers know what's new in it.

(continued)

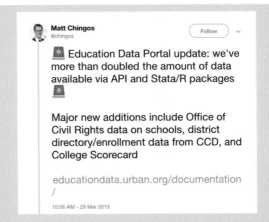

High-profile reporters and researchers often tweet at him about how they use the portal, which proves the target audience found the portal useful. And when the portal entered its beta version, Chingos tweeted out a call for people to test it out and offer feedback. He quickly received responses from willing people interested in education data who he likely wouldn't have reached through cold emails and other traditional channels.

Chingos also uses Twitter to bolster event registration and bring attention to other Urban research, and he engages with people who ask substantive questions about his studies. Educationpolicy discussions can sometimes become contentious, but Chingos avoids confrontations on the platform to maintain a professional but approachable presence.

Chingos has demonstrated that using Twitter for professional connections and circulating his own research, as well as that by his team and others around the world, can help build his profile as an expert in education policy and contribute to the broader research field. He has also shown that asking for feedback from key audiences is another way to leverage a strong social media brand. But it's not all business; Chingos also shares personal stories and experiences to better connect with his Twitter network.

chapter eight

Putting It All Together to Make a Difference

Kate Villarreal

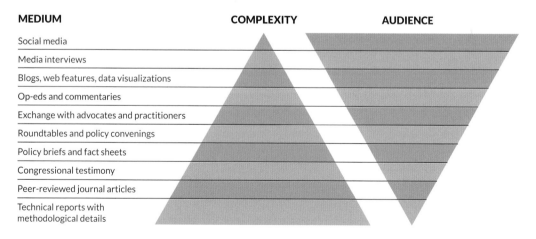

MEDIUM	COMPLEXITY	AUDIENCE
Social media		
Media interviews		
Blogs, web features, data visualizations		
Op-eds and commentaries		
Exchange with advocates and practitioners		
Roundtables and policy convenings		
Policy briefs and fact sheets		
Congressional testimony		
Peer-reviewed journal articles		
Technical reports with methodological details		

Now that you've gotten a taste of all the creative ways to communicate your work, you may be tempted to dive right in and start producing elegant charts, engaging blog posts, and smart tweets. It's natural to gravitate toward the most tangible (and fun) tasks at hand.

Your work will stand a much better chance at making an impact, however, if you step back and think about what you are trying to achieve and how you will get it done. In other words, you need a plan.

In this chapter, I discuss how to build an overarching communications strategy that weaves together the lessons from the previous chapters into a single, focused plan. Taking the time to plan your dissemination approach, rather than jumping into products and tactics, will help you in three ways. First, it will help you set clear goals for communicating your research. Second, it will help you use your resources most efficiently. And third, it will help you know if your strategy was successful.

We'll go step-by-step through the "Policy Impact Plan" worksheet, which you can find at the end of this chapter and on the book's website (https://www.urban.org/ElevatetheDebateBook).

Myth: If You Build It, They Will Come

One of the early mistakes we made at the Urban Institute is believing so strongly in the virtues of our research products that we assumed our audiences would magically find them. We'd get so caught up in the "wow factor" of the research that we'd devote a wildly disproportionate amount of time and resources to creating beautiful products compared with the time we'd spend planning and conducting outreach for those same products.

For example, a researcher could write a report showing a groundbreaking new policy insight. They might even go the extra mile and spend months producing a gorgeous interactive map that lets users take a deep dive into local data around the world. This trailblazing new work is bound to get noticed, right? So, we post the report and map on the Urban website and wait for attention to follow.

Unfortunately, with no further plan to promote and share the work, the insights from that report will have a hard time getting to people beyond our immediate, website "regulars." And if the work goes unnoticed, we could have missed a major opportunity to engage the very actors who could use the analysis to shape programs and policies that affect people's everyday lives.

Start with a Goal

Good communications planning, like any kind of strategic planning exercise, begins with stating a goal.

Policy Impact Plan Template

Plan for: _____

Goal: _____

What is it that you ultimately hope to achieve in sharing your research? Some example goals include:

- Inform a current federal policy debate, such as healthcare reform, immigration policy, or infrastructure spending.
- Become a go-to source for the media in a specific issue area.
- Demonstrate a program model that's working well and encourage others to adopt it.

This is your chance to step back and size up the opportunity: *What are you actually trying to accomplish?*

For some, this can feel more challenging than writing the original research paper. If you find that your brain freezes when faced with aspirational thinking, then my advice is to start small.

Your research doesn't need to immediately change the world, but if it's to have an impact beyond the academic audience or your small sphere, then your goal could be simply to get the work in front of the top two or three people who are best positioned to act upon it.

Remember to keep your goal achievable and measurable. You'll want to be able to look back after your dissemination effort is complete and assess how successful you were.

Identify Your Key Audiences

Next, it's time to think about who needs to see, and ultimately act, on your research so you can achieve your goal (see Chapter 2 on audience development).

> **Identify your key audiences.** Who might benefit from learning about your research?
>
> Audience A
>
> Audience B
>
> Audience C

Although you obviously want everyone to read your paper, that's probably not a realistic goal. Instead, think about who would rise to the top of the list. There could be multiple audiences you want to engage, and each will require a different approach. For example, say you're getting ready to publish an evaluation of a women's jail reentry program in Houston, and your goal is to get people to take notice of it and adopt its model:

- Audience A is reentry program directors throughout Texas.
- Audience B is Texas legislature committee staff who focus on criminal justice issues.
- Audience C is news reporters at the Houston Chronicle.

Prioritizing your audiences from the start will also help you allocate your communications resources most effectively and keep you focused on your goal.

What do you want them to do? What actions might they take after learning about your research?

Audience A _____

Audience B _____

Audience C _____

Next, think about what actions you want each audience to take after they learn about your work.

- Audience A. *Reentry program directors* implement your findings into their programs, invite you to present at their annual conference, and share your work with their peers.
- Audience B. *Legislative staff* invite you to speak at a briefing or give testimony in a hearing, cite your findings in legislation, and view you as a go-to resource on criminal justice issues.
- Audience C. *Reporters* write about your findings, interview and quote you, and view you as a helpful source for future stories.

Taking the time to think about not just who your audience is, but also what you want them to do with your work, will help you articulate the impact you want to have.

Plan Your Timeline

Researchers, and all types of communicators, often underestimate the importance of timing. If you're analyzing the effects of a proposal that policymakers are debating today, your analysis should be in their hands today, if not last week.

Getting your research to people shortly before, or at the moment when it's relevant to their work is fundamental to the success of your communications plan. A research brief on veterans will receive more attention if you release it in the days leading up to or on Veterans Day in November than it would if you release it on a random day in February (unless there happens to be a national conversation on veterans happening in February, in which case, go for it!).

Plan your time. What's the timing for your outreach? Are there key events to keep in mind? Are you working toward a specific deadline?

	Jan	Feb	Mar	Apr	May	Jun	Jul	Aug	Sep	Oct	Nov	Dec
Deliverable 1												
Deliverable 2												

As you plan the timing of your outreach, take a moment to consider key events when your work will be germane. If you want to appeal to state legislators in Texas, then take advantage of the period shortly before or during the state's legislative session, which, in Texas, is just a few weeks every other year. That's when advocates, statehouse reporters, and other influencers are most engaged in these conversations.

Anticipating and planning around key events can also help you identify opportunities in the news cycle that can lift up your work. For example, if you know the next Super Bowl will take place in Miami, Florida, you can predict that news outlets will produce related coverage in the weeks leading up to it.

This would be an optimal time to release related research—maybe that's an analysis of low-income housing challenges in the city of Miami, or perhaps a paper on wage disparities by race in the NFL, or a journal article on concussions and chronic traumatic encephalopathy (CTE). With the Super Bowl as a news hook, reporters will be looking for new and interesting stories to tell. You could be the source that provides that story because you planned ahead and timed things well.

You should also consider the events that could detract from your outreach. We generally avoid promoting research, especially new research, on Fridays, Saturdays, Sundays, holidays, and sometimes even the day before or after a holiday. Even if the product contains a highly attention-grabbing new statistic or insight, it's best to share it with the world during the traditional workweek, when people are most engaged.

What Time of Day?

If news media is your top audience, timing is of the utmost importance, right down to the hour of the day. To increase your chances of securing news coverage of your product on the day it is published, you'll need an interested reporter and a release time that suits that particular news outlet.

For example, if you're working with a reporter from your local radio station who's preparing a story to air during his morning news show, you will need to make sure your work gets published sometime between 12 a.m. and the start of the show. Different outlets require different timing, so it's always best to check with the reporter on what's optimal (see Chapter 6, especially the box on radio and television interviews).

Who Gets an Early Look?

This step is not vital, but as get more experienced conducting outreach, you may develop a short list of people with whom you'll want to share advance copies of your work. These are members of your key audience who get a sneak preview of your research before it's publicly released. This list may include members of the media, influential people in your field, and even potential critics or detractors (see Chapter 2).

Planning a week or even a few days of "embargoed" outreach to reporters can help tremendously if one of your goals is to secure media coverage. Embargoed outreach to other key stakeholders—whether they're people who will help you promote your work or people who may criticize it—can also help increase the chances that it will be positively received.

Everything Old Is New Again

While you should plan the bulk of your outreach around the initial release of your research, your communications planning should factor in a timeline that goes beyond the immediate release so your work doesn't just fade away into the background. For best results, grab a calendar and start making a list of strategic dates. This includes major conferences or other venues where you can give presentations and share your work and when key legislative bodies will be in session.

Anticipate when reporters and social media influencers will be talking about your issues. For example, the week leading up to Mother's Day may be a prime opportunity to recirculate your six-month-old analysis of maternal health in the United States. Your work, if relevant to what people are talking about, need not be "new" to be given new life.

Craft Your Message

Now think about how you want to talk about your research. Having a clear and distilled message will set you up for success on a few fronts. For one, it will be harder for others to misconstrue or misrepresent your insights if you're able to state them plainly. And two, a tight message better lends itself to dissemination across multiple media platforms, some of which require highly abbreviated text (e.g., a 280-character tweet).

To write a compelling message, you should think about the three to five key points that are the most important takeaways from the research. Imagine the newspaper headline you'd like to see about your report. What's the upshot? Why does this research matter? (You might use the presentation worksheet you created in Chapter 4 as a starting point.)

> **Write your key messages.** What is your headline message that will make your audience sit up and take notice? What's new, different, surprising, or challenges expectations?
>
> _____
>
> _____
>
> _____

Example: Key Takeaways for "Evaluation of the Bayou City Women's Reentry Program"

You're about to publish a 150-page report evaluating a program that provides reentry support services for women coming out of the jail system. Your key takeaways should include a short description of what you did, what you learned, and why it matters. It might help to think about this as your "elevator pitch." How would you summarize what you did in 60 seconds or less?

- We just published an evaluation of the Bayou City Women's Reentry Program, a job skills training program that teaches women coming out of jail how to code and build apps.
- We tracked the job placement rate for all graduates and found that 75% were in high-paying technology jobs five years after the program ended.
- To put that in perspective, that's 5,000 women who are supporting themselves and contributing to our tech economy, because they were given an opportunity to learn a new skill.

- Of the remaining 25 percent, 10 percent went to work in minimum-wage jobs and 15 percent returned to incarceration.
- While not everyone went on to find financial success, the important thing to keep in mind is that this program worked for most of the participants. Other cities should explore similar approaches so that we can get more people back to work instead of back to jail.

Think about how to target your message to your top audiences. Reporters, for example, will want to know what's new about what you've uncovered. What makes this work interesting and worthy of news coverage? What kind of superlatives can you use to describe it? Is it the first time this work has been done? Is this the largest, most rigorous study of its kind? Did you use data that's never been analyzed before?

If the work you're releasing is national in scale, pull out local insights when talking with local audiences. Policymakers may be curious about what makes the work unique, but they'll also want to know how it affects the people who live in their home districts. Your conversations with them should lead with data or findings that are most relevant to their states. They'll also want to know the policy implications or recommendations.

The same applies for engaging with local media outlets. The public radio station in Tucson, Arizona may be interested in a national report on how the U.S. population is aging, but they'll be most curious to know what it means for senior citizens in Tucson and the state of Arizona.

Identify Your Messengers

Once you have a clear message, think about who you can engage to help you deliver it more broadly. This would include key influencers mentioned earlier and really anyone with credibility and a connection to one of your audiences who can be your cheerleader (recall this graphic from Chapter 2). These are your messengers.

CONCEPTUALIZING YOUR AUDIENCE

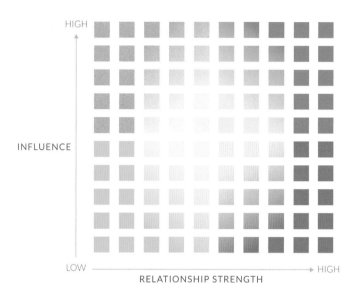

INFLUENCE

HIGH

LOW   RELATIONSHIP STRENGTH   HIGH

INFLUENCERS

Inform with relevant, timely, useful information

Direct email, events, and retail engagement

KEY STAKEHOLDERS

Keep informed with regular, personal contact; enlist strategically

Personal email, speaker requests, and in-person engagement

FAN CLUB

Keep informed and engaged; enlist periodically

Newsletters, social media, and events

OTHERS

Keep Informed

Newsletters and social media

In addition to sharing an advance copy of the research, you can also provide them with a package of materials to help you spread the word. That package could include your key takeaways, sample language, and graphics for social media promotion. If you make it easy for your messengers, they will want to help you promote your work.

Choose Your Communication Tactics

Now it's finally time to get tactical. Returning to your audience list (which you hopefully started developing in Chapter 2), what are the best ways to reach them?

List your channels and tactics. How can you reach your audiences?

Audience A _____

Audience B _____

Audience C _____

Let's say your goal is to get more programs to follow the model of the Bayou City Women's Reentry Program.

Here are suggested tactics:

- Audience A. *Reentry program directors*: Send a direct email, target them with social media content, invite them to a reentry-themed webinar.
- Audience B. *Legislative staff who work on criminal justice*: Send a direct email, place an op-ed in the capital city newspaper.
- Audience C. *Reporters*: Email a short media pitch note or invite them to a public event where you'll speak about the work.

You can also ask others for help reaching these different audiences. Does your organization or university have a media or outreach department that can help you? Do you have a friend or colleague who has connections to some of your target groups? The other chapters in this book can help you devise specific strategies for presentations, talking to reporters, blog writing, and social media platforms.

Plan and Create Your Products

Be mindful of how to best package your publication for different audiences and for their respective outreach channels. This may require creating supplementary products that distill your work into more digestible formats.

If your core research report is 150 pages, produce a two-page executive summary, a single-page fact sheet, or even an infographic or simple graph. Short summary documents are highly useful to the busy policy staffer looking for key takeaways or the journalist who wants to get a general sense of your report before deciding whether it's worth her time.

Prepare your messengers. Are there validators, thought leaders, influencers, etc., who can help you carry your message? Are there materials that you need to create to help share your message?

❑ Fact sheet   ❑ Media pitch   ❑ Tweet

❑ Written testimony   ❑ Elevator pitch   ❑ LinkedIn post/blog

❑ Policy brief   ❑ Blog post   ❑ Facebook message

❑ Other:

If you're pursuing a social media strategy, this absolutely requires some forethought and attention to supplemental products (see Chapter 7). For example, if you tweet a link to your 150-page report, it's very unlikely that one of your Twitter followers will, upon clicking the link, drop everything and read it.

For social media channels like Facebook and Twitter, it's more effective to create and share content that grabs the attention and can be accessed quickly. That might be a compelling chart or an image that states a key finding. Or you can author a 400- to 800-word blog post and link to it in your tweet or post. It stands a much greater chance of being consumed than a long report.

For engaging traditional news media, you'll need to write a short note—a media pitch—that distills your work into interesting and scannable bullet points along with any compelling charts or visuals. Contacting reporters with a heads-up in the weeks or days leading up to a release can often work in your favor.

If you decide to use a media embargo period, you'll need to have an early shareable version of your product that you can send to the reporter. If the product is still going through minor copyedits and formatting, you may want to watermark it with the word "DRAFT" and indicate the date and time the embargo will lift.

Remember that every product, even that 280-character tweet, should draw from your foundation of research, as discussed in Chapter 1 and drawn upon throughout the previous chapters.

In creating these products, you are not dumbing down your research; instead, you are taking the most salient points and shaping them into a product that will best lend itself to a particular communications channel. Your reward is that you will ultimately reach your audience in the most effective way.

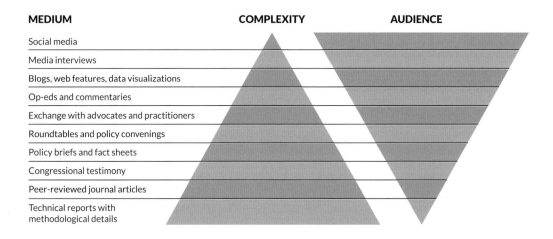

MEDIUM	COMPLEXITY	AUDIENCE
Social media		
Media interviews		
Blogs, web features, data visualizations		
Op-eds and commentaries		
Exchange with advocates and practitioners		
Roundtables and policy convenings		
Policy briefs and fact sheets		
Congressional testimony		
Peer-reviewed journal articles		
Technical reports with methodological details		

Measure Your Impact

The final step is deciding how you will evaluate the success of your effort. Look at your goal and think about how you will measure your progress. Did you successfully reach the audiences you identified, and did they take the actions you wanted them to take?

Evaluate. How will you know whether your plan was successful? How will you measure outputs and outcomes?

_____

_____

_____

Returning to the example of the Bayou City program, how will you know if your work was able to break through to your three audiences? This could be measured by:

- *Program directors and legislative staff:* The number of responses you got to your direct emails, the number of attendees at your webinar, invitations to come speak or engage further.
- *Journalists:* The number of resulting media stories and quality of the coverage, including quotes and links to your research.
- *All three audiences:* The number of times your product or related news coverage was shared on social media and follow-up calls seeking your expertise.

You can look globally at all three audiences and assess their engagement levels. Were any of them sharing your work on social media or referencing it at public events or in media interviews? If you didn't know them already, did your initial contact with these audiences sow the seeds for longer-term relationships and future collaborations?

Depending on how sophisticated your digital communications strategy is, you can also use site traffic measurement tools to gather data on items like total page views, total publication downloads, average time on page, and more. If you use a social media strategy, there are various tools to measure how well your social posts performed and how often people shared and engaged with your content (see Chapter 7).

Wrapping Up

Smart communications planning always starts with a goal. Be clear and focused about what you're ultimately trying to achieve. This requires thinking about who your audience is, how to reach them, and what you'd like them to do with your work. Then you can plan your timeline and tactics, including the messages you're trying to get across about your research.

What are the three or four key takeaways you want to make at every opportunity, whether it's a media interview, a presentation, a series of tweets, or a quick elevator pitch? Think about other people in your field who can help amplify those messages and widen your reach.

Choose the communications channels to reach your audience and repackage your work into the formats best suited to those channels. As you plan your outreach timeline, keep in mind relevant opportunities that can help boost visibility for your research and then leverage those opportunities. Last, you'll want to figure out how to measure whether you've achieved your goal and how to track the impact of your efforts.

Taking the time to think through a policy impact plan will help set your work up for maximum visibility and engagement from your target audiences. And you can always scale down or up, depending on individual projects and goals. The worksheet we just went through can be customized for a project with a $2 million budget, a $200 budget, or even a $2 budget. And no matter what level of resources are available to you—a full-size communications team or a one-person shoestring operation—you should always take the time to think through what you're actually trying to accomplish and how you're going to get there.

Key Takeaways

- Thoughtful planning helps set your work up for maximum visibility and engagement from the audiences you care about most.
- Taking the time to fill out a policy impact plan worksheet will help you see how your products and tactics can work together in a cohesive strategy to achieve your goal.
- Each step of your plan, from deciding the timing of your release to which communications channels and products you'll use, should focus on how to best reach your target audience.
- Having a plan will also help you look back and assess where your strategy was successful and where you should adjust for the next time around.

Policy Impact Plan Template

Plan for: _____

Goal: _____

Identify your key audiences. Who might benefit from learning about your research?

Audience A _____

Audience B _____

Audience C _____

What do you want them to do? What actions might they take after learning about your research?

Audience A _____

Audience B _____

Audience C _____

(*continued*)

Plan your time. What's the timing for your outreach? Are there key events to keep in mind? Are you working toward a specific deadline?

	Jan	Feb	Mar	Apr	May	Jun	Jul	Aug	Sep	Oct	Nov	Dec
Deliverable 1												
Deliverable 2												

Write your key messages. What is your headline message that will make your audience sit up and take notice? What's new, different, surprising, or challenges expectations?

_____

_____

List your channels and tactics. How can you reach your audiences?

Audience A _____

Audience B _____

Audience C _____

Prepare your messengers. Are there validators, thought leaders, influencers, etc. who can help you carry your message? Are there materials that you need to create to help share your message?

❑ Fact sheet   ❑ Media pitch   ❑ Tweet
❑ Written testimony   ❑ Elevator pitch   ❑ LinkedIn post/blog
❑ Policy brief   ❑ Blog post   ❑ Facebook message
❑ Other:

Evaluate. How will you know whether your plan was successful? How will you measure outputs and outcomes?

_____

_____

Case Study: *Developing structures and processes for a robust communications team*

Throughout this book, we've shown that good research communication is hard to do alone. Urban's team may serve as a good model for how to build your organization's communications capabilities. Our communications team, which has grown dramatically over the past five years, now consists of more than 50 people. As our efforts have paid off, our organization has prioritized its emphasis on better research communication.

The team is split across eight groups:

1. Digital Communications: develops and maintains the website and digital content.
2. Editorial Services: provides copyediting and other editorial support for all materials.
3. External Affairs: links Urban's researchers with decisionmakers, policymakers, and other groups through direct outreach.
4. Strategic Communications: leads strategies that raise the visibility of research and engage critical audiences through media and other outreach. Many of these team members are embedded within Urban's research centers.
5. Visual Communications: maintains Urban's visual brand and designs digital and print products.
6. Writing Services: provides direct writing support for digital features, reports, and more.
7. Data Visualization: creates static and interactive graphs for a variety of Urban products.
8. Operations: leads project management, coordination, and administration.

Staff in these groups frequently collaborate to execute a communications strategy for each research product. Our broader communications team has undergone many iterations of how these groups are organized. Your organization may not need all these groups, so you should decide what structure works best.

(continued)

Our communications team also uses regular meetings and tools to help coordinate efforts across the internal groups and across research centers.

- Stand-Up Meeting: Three mornings each week, the entire communications team meets for 15 minutes to discuss upcoming report releases, blog posts, outreach efforts, newsletters, and other goings-on to make sure everyone is aware of what is happening across the organization. To help keep the meeting short, everyone stands. The information lives in an online project management database and on a whiteboard wall in the physical center of the department to track everything for the week.
- Intake Forms: To obtain communications support, researchers must fill out an online form (hosted on an Urban intranet page) with information about their research's target audience, publication type, target date, funder, and more.
- Kickoff Meeting: After a communications team has been assigned to a research project through the intake process, staff members meet with the researchers to discuss what the product could look like, key audiences, and next steps.
- Biweekly Reports: Every two weeks, team members update a document detailing the highlights of recent communications efforts, new initiatives under way, hiring announcements, and other relevant information for Urban's president and executive team.
- Slack Channel: Urban's team uses the Slack messaging service to communicate quickly throughout the day. Some discussion may be fun or trivial, such as when leftover food is available, but other channels are dedicated to the blog, visuals, editing, and more.

Your organization may not need all these tools and meetings. But after much trial and error, we have found these practices serve our needs and ensure our team can help researchers achieve their communications goals.

Bibliography

Chapter 1 Why Research Needs a Big Audience

Alda, Alan. *If I Understood You, Would I Have This Look on My Face? My Adventures in the Art and Science of Relating and Communicating.* New York: Random House Trade Paperbacks, 2018.

Bump, Philip. "Reminder: It's Very Unusual to Vote on a Health-Care Bill Before Congress Knows What It Will Do." *The Washington Post* (September 19, 2017). https://www.washingtonpost.com/news/politics/wp/2017/09/19/reminder-its-very-unusual-to-vote-on-a-health-care-bill-before-congress-knows-what-it-will-do/.

Delistraty, Cody C. "The Psychological Comforts of Storytelling." *Harvard Business Review* (November 2, 2014).

Fingerhut, Hannah. "Republicans Skeptical of Colleges' Impact on U.S., but Most See Benefits for Workforce Participation." *FactTank: News in the Numbers.* Pew Research Center (July 20, 2017).

Gallup. "Military, Small Business, Police Stir Most Confidence." (June 28, 2018). https://news.gallup.com/poll/236243/military-small-business-police-stir-confidence.aspx.

Harrington, Matthews. "Survey: People's Trust Has Declined in Business, Media, Government, and NGOs." *Harvard Business Review* (January 16, 2017).

Mance, Henry. "Britain Has Had Enough of Experts, Says Gove." *Financial Times* (June 3, 2016).

Medina, John. *Brain Rules: 12 Principles for Surviving and Thriving at Work, Home, and School.* Seattle WA: Pear Press, 2014.

NPR/PBS NewsHour/Marist Poll Results (January, 2018). http://maristpoll.marist.edu/nprpbs-newshourmarist-poll-results-january-2018/.

Pew Research Center. "Public Confidence in Scientists Has Remained Stable for Decades." (March 22, 2019). https://www.pewresearch.org /fact-tank/2019/03/22/public-confidence-in-scientists-has-remained -stable-for-decades/.

Stein, Jeff. "House Republicans: The CBO Will Back Us Up. And It Doesn't Matter If It Doesn't." *Vox Media* (March 8, 2017).

Zak, Paul J. "How Stories Change the Brain." *Greater Good Magazine* (December 17, 2013).

Zak, Paul J. "Why Your Brain Loves Good Storytelling." *Harvard Business Review* (October 28, 2014).

Chapter 2 Developing an Audience Outreach Strategy

Governing the States and Localities. "Federal Employees by State." (January 19, 2018). http://www.governing.com/gov-data/federal -employees-workforce-numbers-by-state.html.

Chapter 3 An Introduction to Visualizing Your Research

Note: The content in this chapter is largely drawn from the author's book, *Better Presentations: A Guide for Scholars, Researchers, and Wonks* and his 2014 article in the *Journal of Economic Perspectives*, "An Economist's Guide to Visualizing Data."

Few, Stephen. "Tapping the Power of Visual Perception." *Visual Business Intelligence Newsletter* (September 4, 2004). http://www.perceptualedge .com/articles/ie/visual_perception.pdf.

Healey, Christopher G., and James T. Enns. "Attention and Visual Memory in Visualization and Computer Graphics." *IEEE Transactions on Visualization and Computer Graphics* 18, no. 7 (2012): 1170–1188.

Kosara, Robert, and Jock Mackinlay. "Storytelling: The Next Step for Visualization." *Computer* 46, no. 5 (2013): 44–50.

Schwabish, Jonathan. "An Economist's Guide to Visualizing Data." *Journal of Economic Perspectives* 28, no. 1 (Winter 2014): 209–234.

Schwabish, Jonathan. *Better Presentations: A Guide for Scholars, Researchers, and Wonks.* New York: Columbia University Press, 2016.

Segel, Edward, and Jeffrey Heer. "Narrative Visualization: Telling Stories with Data." *IEEE Transactions on Visualization and Computer Graphics* 16, no. 6 (2010): 1139–1148.

Social Security Advisory Board. "Aspects of Disability Decision Making: Data and Materials." Social Security Administration (February 2012). http://www.ssab.gov/Publications/Disability/GPO_Chartbook_FINAL _06122012.pdf.

Szucs, Kristina. "Spotlight on Profitability." Infographic (2012). http://krisztinaszucs.com/my-product/hollywood/.

Chapter 4 Better Presentations: More Effective Speaking

Note: The content in this chapter is largely drawn from the author's book, *Better Presentations: A Guide for Scholars, Researchers, and Wonks.*

Mayer, Richard. *Multimedia Learning.* New York: Cambridge University Press, 2009.

Paivio, Alan. *Mental Representations: A Dual Coding Approach.* Oxford: Oxford University Press, 1986.

Paivio, Alan. *Images in Mind: The Evolution of a Theory.* New York: Harvester Wheatsheaf, 1991.

Sweller, John, Paul Ayres, and Slava Kalyuga. *Cognitive Load Theory.* 11th ed. New York: Springer, 2011.

Chapter 5 How to Blog about Your Findings

Akers, Beth, and Matthew M. Chingos. *Game of Loans: The Rhetoric and Reality of Student Debt.* Princeton, NJ: Princeton University Press, 2016.

Bergstrom, Breonna. "How Long Should a Blog Post Be to Get the Most Traffic and Shares?" *CoSchedule* (January 8, 2018). https://blog.bufferapp .com/optimal-length-social-media.

Costill, Albert. "50 Things You Should Know About Tumblr." *Search Engine Journal* (January 9, 2014). https://www.searchenginejournal.com/50- things-know-tumblr/84595/.

Fifield, Adam. "5 Tips for Google's New Meta Title Guidelines in 2018." *Big Leap* (December 20, 2017). https://www.bigleap.com/blog/5-tips -take-advantage-googles-new-meta-title-guidelines-2016/.

Jane, Talia. "An Open Letter to My CEO." *Medium* (February 19, 2016). https://medium.com/@taliajane/an-open-letter-to-my-ceo-fb73df021e7a.

Jeffries, Adrianne. "Posterous Is Shutting Down: Here Are the Best Alternatives." *The Verge* (April 30, 2013). https://www.theverge .com/2013/4/30/4281780/posterous-is-shutting-down-tomorrow -here-are-the-best-alternatives.

Kooragayala, Shiva, and Tanaya Srini. "Pokémon GO Is Changing How Cities Use Public Space, but Could It Be More Inclusive?" *Urban Wire* (August 1, 2016). https://www.urban.org/urban-wire /pokemon-go-changing-how-cities-use-public-space-could-it-be -more-inclusive.

Lee, Kevan. "Infographic: The Optimal Length for Every Social Media Update and More." *Buffer* (October 21, 2014). https://blog.bufferapp .com/optimal-length-social-media.

National Journal Leadership Council. "Media Habits of Congressional Staff in the Digital Age: Insights from the 2017 Washington in the Information Age Study." (February 28, 2018). http://go.nationaljournal.com/rs/556 -YEE-969/images/Media-Habits-of-Congressional-Staff-in-the-Digital -Age_2.28.2018.pdf.

National Journal Leadership Council. "How Washington Insiders Get Their Information: Insights from Washington in the Information Age 2018." (November 2018).

Rao, Shebani, and Nancy G. La Vigne. "Five Ways to Reduce Crime." *Urban Wire* (May 8, 2013). https://www.urban.org/urban-wire/five-ways -reduce-crime.

Simms, Margaret. "Visibility for Women of Color Is the Crucial First Step toward Equality." *Urban Wire* (March 8, 2018). https://www .urban.org/urban-wire/visibility-women-color-crucial-first-step -toward-equality.

Snow, Shane. "This Surprising Reading Level Analysis Will Change the Way You Write." *The Content Strategist* (January 28, 2015). https://contently .com/2015/01/28/this-surprising-reading-level-analysis-will-change -the-way-you-write/.

Sussman, Ed. "The New Rules of Social Journalism: A Proposal." *Pando* (March 29, 2014). https://pando.com/2014/03/29/the-new-rules-of -social-journalism-a-proposal/.

Tumblr. About page. Accessed December 2019. https://www.tumblr .com/about.

Chapter 6 Working with the Media to Increase Your Impact

Jan, Tracy. "White Families Have Nearly 10 Times the Net Worth of Black Families. And the Gap Is Growing." *Washington Post* (September 28, 2017). https://www.washingtonpost.com/news/wonk/wp/2017/09/28 /black-and-hispanic-families-are-making-more-money-but-they-still -lag-far-behind-whites/.

Jan, Tracy. "Here's Why the Wealth Gap Is Widening Between White
  Families and Everyone Else." *Washington Post* (October 5, 2017).
  https://www.washingtonpost.com/news/wonk/wp/2017/10/05
  /heres-why-the-wealth-gap-is-widening-between-white-families-and
  -everyone-else/.

Kijakazi, Kilolo and Heather McCulloch. "Building Women's Wealth Is
  Key to Economic Security." (May 29, 2018). https://slate.com/human
  -interest/2018/05/gender-inequality-closing-the-wealth-gap-is-critical
  -to-future-financial-security.html.

La Ferla, Ruth. "The Captionfluencers." *New York Times* (March 27, 2019).
  https://www.nytimes.com/2019/03/27/style/instagram-long-captions
  .html.

LaVito, Angelica. "Tax Reform Was Hard for Reagan in 1986. It Might Be
  Even Harder for Trump Today." *CNBC* (August 16, 2017). https://www
  .cnbc.com/2017/08/16/reagan-tax-reform-approved-by-congress-in
  -1986-harder-for-trump-now.html.

Shen, Lucinda. "Why Some Investors Are Refusing to Buy Walmart
  Stock." *Fortune* (March 5, 2018). http://fortune.com/2018/03/05
  /walmart-guns-kroger-parkland-florida-shooting-blackrock
  -vanguard/.

Woodall, Marian K. *How to Think on Your Feet*. New York: Warner
  Books, 1993.

Yang, Jenny. "Does the law protect the LGBTQ community from
  discrimination? It should be an easy answer." (April 26, 2019).
  https://www.washingtonpost.com/opinions/2019/04/26/does-law
  -protect-lgbtq-community-discrimination-it-should-be-an-
  easy-answer/.

Chapter 7 Social Media Can Build Audiences That Matter

Ali, Raian, Emily Arden-Close, and John McAlaney. "Digital Addiction:
  How Technology Keeps Us Hooked." *The Conversation* (June 12, 2018).
  https://theconversation.com/digital-addiction-how-technology-keeps
  -us-hooked-97499.

"Digital Addiction Research." Bournemouth University. Accessed April
  2019. https://research.bournemouth.ac.uk/project/dar/.

Flaiz, William. "Universal Search Should Be a Plus." *Search Engine
  Watch* (December 8, 2008). https://searchenginewatch.com/sew
  /news/2064364/universal-search-should-be-plus.

Meshi, Dar, Anastassia Elizarova, Andrew Bender, and Antonio Verdejo-Garcia. "Excessive Social Media Users Demonstrate Impaired Decision Making in the Iowa Gambling Task." *Journal of Behavioral Addictions* 8, no. 1 (2019): 169–173.

National Journal. "Washington in the Information Age 2017." Accessed August 2018. https://www.nationaljournal.com/bp/659170/washington-information-age.

Newport, Cal. *Digital Minimalism: On Living Better with Less Technology.* New York: Portfolio, 2019.

Case Studies

Acs, Gregory, Laura Wheaton, and Elaine Waxman. "Assessing Changes to SNAP Work Requirements in the 2018 Farm Bill." *Urban Institute* (May 15, 2018). https://www.urban.org/research/publication/assessing-changes-snap-work-requirements-2018-farm-bill.

Cunningham, Mary K., et al. "A Pilot Study of Landlord Acceptance of Housing Choice Vouchers." *Urban Institute* (August 20, 2018a). https://www.urban.org/research/publication/pilot-study-landlord-acceptance-housing-choice-vouchers.

Cunningham, Mary, and Martha Galvez. "State Policymakers Are Making Affordable Housing Problems Worse in Texas." *TribTalk* (April 17, 2019). https://www.tribtalk.org/2019/04/17/state-policymakers-are-making-affordable-housing-problems-worse-in-texas/.

Cunningham, Mary K., Martha M. Galvez, and Emily Peiffer. "Landlords Limit Voucher Holders' Choice in Where They Can Live." *Urban Wire* (August 20, 2018). https://www.urban.org/urban-wire/landlords-limit-voucher-holders-choice-where-they-can-live.

Hahn, Heather. "That's Scary: America Spends as Much on Halloween as It Does on Head Start." *Urban Wire* (October 31, 2017). https://www.urban.org/urban-wire/thats-scary-america-spends-much-halloween-it-does-head-start.

Hahn, Heather, Eleanor Pratt, Eva Allen, Genevieve Kenney, Diane K. Levy, and Elaine Waxman. "Work Requirements in Social Safety Net Programs: A Status Report of Work Requirements in TANF, SNAP, Housing Assistance, and Medicaid." *Urban Institute* (December 22, 2017). https://www.urban.org/research/publication/work-requirements-social-safety-net-programs-status-report-work-requirements-tanf-snap-housing-assistance-and-medicaid.

Isaacs, Julia, et al. "Kids' Share 2017: Report on Federal Expenditures on Children through 2016 and Future Projections." *Urban Institute* (October 31, 2017). https://www.urban.org/research/publication/kids-share-2017-report-federal-expenditures-children-through-2016-and-future-projections.

Karpman, Michael, Stephen Zuckerman, and Dulce Gonzalez. "Material Hardship among Nonelderly Adults and Their Families in 2017." *Urban Institute* (August 28, 2018). https://www.urban.org/research /publication/material-hardship-among-nonelderly-adults-and-their -families-2017.

Oneto, Alyse D., Martha M. Galvez, and Claudia Aranda. "Los Angeles County Is Taking Steps to Prevent Discrimination against Housing Voucher Holders." *Urban Wire* (February 15, 2019). https://www .urban.org/urban-wire/los-angeles-county-taking-steps-prevent -discrimination-against-housing-voucher-holders.

Oneto, Alyse D., Emily Peiffer, Claudia Aranda, and Martha M. Galvez. "Despite the Law, Landlords Still Reject Voucher Holders in DC." *Urban Institute* (September 20, 2018). https://greaterdc.urban.org/blog /despite-law-landlords-still-reject-voucher-holders-dc.

Urban Institute. "Education Data Explorer Beta." Accessed October 2019. https://educationdata.urban.org/data-explorer/.

Urban Institute. "Nine Charts about Wealth Inequality in America." (October 5, 2017). https://apps.urban.org/features/wealth -inequality-charts/.

Urban Institute. "From Safety Net to Solid Ground." Accessed October 2019. https://www.urban.org/features/safety-net-solid-ground.

Urban Institute. "The Well-Being and Basic Needs Survey." (various years). Accessed October 2019. https://www.urban.org/policy-centers/health -policy-center/projects/well-being-and-basic-needs-survey.

Urban Institute. "Housing Finance Policy Center." Accessed October 2019. https://www.urban.org/policy-centers/housing-finance-policy-center /projects/housing-finance-glance-monthly-chartbooks.

About the Contributors

David Connell is the senior director of digital communications for the Urban Institute. His team is responsible for all aspects of the organization's digital outreach strategy. This includes providing strategic direction for websites and applications; creating content for sites and applications; and crafting distribution strategies through email newsletters, social media, and advertising. Before joining the Urban Institute, Connell worked in various digital communications roles for The Nature Conservancy, the Ocean Conservancy, and the American Society of Landscape Architects.

Amy Elsbree is senior director of external affairs at the Urban Institute. She oversees relationships with Urban's key external audiences: Capitol Hill, the federal executive branch, state and local governments, the business community, the academic community, and other organizations with which Urban shares policy interests. She ensures that their perspectives inform Urban's research agenda and that Urban's research informs state, local, and federal policy discussions. In addition, Elsbree oversees Urban's public events and convenings. Before joining Urban, Elsbree was director of public affairs and member relations at the National League of Cities, where she managed strategic communications, corporate relations, and member relations. Previously, she was director of the Academy for State and Local Government and held various government affairs and communications positions at Amtrak. Early in her career, she worked for the

Office of Federal Relations for the Commonwealth of Massachusetts and on Capitol Hill.

Laura Greenback is a member of Urban Institute's writing services team. She is responsible for coordinating and writing content for the organization's robust newsletter program. She also writes and substantively edits overviews, factsheets, and other publications to ensure that Urban's research findings are accessible to a broad range of audiences. Before coming to Urban, Greenback was communications director at the Software & Information Industry Association, where she promoted policy positions on behalf of member companies including Google, IBM, and Bloomberg. She has a BA in English from Washington College and an MA in interactive journalism from American University.

Serena Lei is director of writing services at the Urban Institute. She oversees a team of writers who help create and substantively edit content for all Urban products, including features, blog posts, publications, newsletters, and the website. Before joining Urban, Lei was a reporter. She received her bachelor's degree from Johns Hopkins University and her master's degree from Northwestern University's Medill School of Journalism.

Stu Kantor managed media relations for the Urban Institute until 2019. He came to Urban in 2002 after 18 years with the Public Broadcasting Service, where he served as the director of PBS corporate communications and as the director of creative communications and editorial services for PBS Businesses. Kantor has been a researcher-reporter at WETA-TV in Washington, DC, for *The Lawmakers*, a weekly PBS series on Congress; the research and talent coordinator for *Why in the World*, a PBS current-affairs series for high school students; and a reporter for newspapers in New York, New Mexico, and Iowa. He earned a BA in English and linguistics from the University of Rochester and an MA in political science from American University.

Bridget Lowell is the chief communications officer and vice president for communications at the Urban Institute. She joined Urban in 2012, bringing with her more than 15 years of experience across the nonprofit and private sectors, Capitol Hill, and the media industry. Before joining Urban, Lowell served as director of strategic communications at The Nature Conservancy, the world's leading environmental conservation organization. In this capacity, she was known for her work in media relations, reputation management, and strengthening organizational brand identity. Lowell also worked for nearly five years on Capitol Hill as communications director for a senior member of Congress from North Carolina; during that time, she completed stints for local and national political campaigns. She began her career as an on-air television news reporter, working first at a cable network in New York's Hudson Valley and later at the ABC affiliate in Winston-Salem, North Carolina. Lowell graduated from Cornell University.

Nicole Levins is senior digital communications manager at the Urban Institute, focused on elevating the organization's profile among online audiences. She oversees and supports content strategy for Urban's social media accounts, *Urban Wire*, Urban.org, newsletters, and online advertising. Before joining Urban, Levins served as The Nature Conservancy's online media relations manager and completed several internships in entertainment media. She majored in professional writing/journalism at The College of New Jersey and has a master's degree in digital communication from the Johns Hopkins University.

Amy Peake is director of government affairs at the Urban Institute. She works with Urban's experts to facilitate conversations and connections with policymakers, including Capitol Hill, the federal executive branch, and state and local government leaders. Before joining Urban, Peake worked as congressional staff for nearly eight years in policy and communications positions. Most recently, she worked for the U.S. House Committee on Education and Labor following positions in a district office and a congressional DC office. Peake started her career working in a city manager's office in Northern California and studied at the University of California, Davis.

Emily Peiffer is a member of the Urban Institute's writing services team and is responsible for reporting and writing feature stories to share Urban insights with a broad audience. She also writes and provides substantive editing for blog posts, reports, and other Urban content. Peiffer previously worked for Industry Dive's *Construction Dive* online news publication, Lancaster Newspapers, and the American Association for the Advancement of Science. She received a bachelor's degree from Susquehanna University.

Jonathan Schwabish is a senior fellow in the Income and Benefits Policy Center at the Urban Institute. He also specializes in data visualization and presentation design as a member of the communications team. His research agenda includes earnings and income inequality, immigration, disability insurance, retirement security, data measurement, and the Supplemental Nutrition Assistance Program. Schwabish is considered a leader in the data visualization field and is a leading voice for clarity and accessibility in research. He has written on various aspects of how to best visualize data, including technical aspects of creation, design best practices, and how to communicate social science research in more accessible ways. He is the author of *Better Presentations: A Guide for Scholars, Researchers, and Wonks*, which helps people improve the way they prepare, design, and deliver data-rich content.

Kate Villarreal is the director of strategic communications for the Urban Institute. She works in close partnership with research and communications staff to lead and execute strategies that raise the visibility of research, engage critical audiences, and help drive smart evidence-based policy. Villarreal joined Urban after serving two years in the Obama administration as public and media affairs staff for former U.S. Trade Representative Ron Kirk. Before this, she pursued graduate study in political communication while managing communications for a nonprofit organization in the Texas Hill Country, where she wrote a weekly news column for the local paper. From 2003 to 2007, Villarreal was a community organizer in Seattle and earned citywide recognition for leading an effort to preserve public housing at Yesler Terrace.

Index